Youth
SOCCER
Drills

Second edition

Jim Garland

Physical Education Instructor
Coordinator of Motion Concepts Soccer Camps

HUMAN KINETICS

Library of Congress Cataloging-in-Publication Data

Garland, Jim, 1948-
  Youth soccer drills / Jim Garland.-- 2nd ed.
    p. cm.
  ISBN 0-7360-5063-9 (soft cover)
  1. Soccer for children--Training. I. Title.
  GV944.2.G37 2003
  796.334'083--dc21

                    2003002117

ISBN-10: 0-7360-5063-9
ISBN-13: 978-0-7360-5063-0

Copyright © 2003, 1997 by Human Kinetics, Inc.

Acquisitions Editor: Dean Miller; **Production Editor:** Melinda Graham; **Assistant Editor:** John Wentworth; **Copyeditor:** Kathy Calder; **Proofreader:** Sarah Wiseman; **Graphic Designer:** Robert Reuther; **Photo Manager:** Dan Wendt; **Cover Designer:** Keith Blomberg, **Photographer (cover):** Leslie A. Woodrum; **Photographer (interior):** pages 1, 151, and 203, Human Kinetics; pages 37 and 69, Greg Philpott; page 133, EMPICS; page 189, Jennifer Smith; **Illustrators:** Susan Carson, Debra Garland; **Printer:** Versa Press

Human Kinetics books are available at special discounts for bulk purchase. Special editions or book excerpts can also be created to specification. For details, contact the Special Sales Manager at Human Kinetics.

Printed in the United States of America   20   19   18   17   16   15   14   13   12

The paper in this book is certified under a sustainable forestry program.

Human Kinetics
Web site: www.HumanKinetics.com

United States: Human Kinetics
P.O. Box 5076
Champaign, IL 61825-5076
800-747-4457
e-mail: humank@hkusa.com

Canada: Human Kinetics
475 Devonshire Road, Unit 100
Windsor, ON N8Y 2L5
800-465-7301 (in Canada only)
e-mail: info@hkcanada.com

Europe: Human Kinetics
107 Bradford Road
Stanningley
Leeds LS28 6AT, United Kingdom
+44 (0)113 255 5665
e-mail: hk@hkeurope.com

Australia: Human Kinetics
57A Price Avenue
Lower Mitcham, South Australia 5062
08 8372 0999
e-mail: info@hkaustralia.com

New Zealand: Human Kinetics
P.O. Box 80
Torrens Park, South Australia 5062
0800 222 062
e-mail: info@hknewzealand.com

Acknowledgments

Thanks to all of my fellow teachers, coaches, and clinicians, especially Jeffrey Tipping and the staff at the National Soccer Coaches Association of America, who have been willing to share their ideas while helping to educate me in the game of soccer. A special thanks to Rob Bailey, who over the years has been a special friend and of great value in helping me develop new teaching strategies. Thanks to Sharon Mitchell for her continued professional assistance with technological issues and typing manuscripts. I would also like to thank Linda Duncan for her editing efforts on this and other projects over the years. And a special thanks to my wife, Debra, for her support and contribution of artwork for this book.

Finally, I would like to dedicate this book to my sons, Casey and Matthew, who are grown men now. Thank you for being my favorite playmates and greatest teachers.

Contents

3

Passing and Collecting Drills 69

4

Heading Drills 133

5

Shooting Drills 151

6

Game Progressions 189

7

Using Drills in Practice 203

Introduction

When I was a child, I loved playing. I was the kind of kid who hated rainy days and got angry when the sun went down in the evening. I still do. Rain or darkness meant playing would have to wait until another day. I was active, very active. I'm still active. Being still was for someone else. Being still meant being bored. None of that for me.

As I grew into adulthood and considered future employment, I knew I wanted two things: to stay active in sports and to help young people experience the same joys I had while at play. Being an elementary physical education teacher and coach was a natural fit for me. I've been teaching for over 30 years now, and I've coached from clinic-level teams through high school boys' varsity sports. In that time I've discovered two things about working with kids: They want to have fun, and if they don't understand what you're talking about, it's probably not their fault.

When working with children as a physical education teacher and coach, I've tried to remember how I felt as a child. I remember how much I hated listening to a coach talk for 20 minutes and then getting to play for only 10 minutes. Standing in long lines waiting for a turn during drills absolutely frazzled me.

These thoughts helped inspire me to write this book. I wanted to give youth soccer coaches a resource filled with activities that are easy to explain and fun, keeping even the most active child satisfied. The drills I selected for this book meet these criteria. Besides providing drills to improve skill techniques, I have heavily emphasized movement concepts to help improve the quality of players' movements. I have designed these drills for coaches of players aged 5 through 12. Players' parents and physical education instructors will also find this a handy reference.

The book is divided into seven chapters. It begins with a chapter on space and movement that discusses open, closed, personal, and general space. These ideas are integrated with concepts of vision, direction, speed, and level into drills that promote the development of efficient movement. This chapter is designed exclusively for players in the 5- to 6-year-old range. Chapters 2 through 5 offer drills dealing with skill acquisition and tactical development. Drills are organized in a progression from least to most challenging. Drills that are least challenging will require less movement. Players often learn skills more quickly by practicing from a stationary position. As players become more successful, drills become more challenging. The coach can introduce movement, change the responsibility of players, or restrict time, space, or touches. The coach can add defensive pressure, beginning with subtle pressure and progressing to gamelike pressure. These chapters include drills that develop skills in dribbling, passing, collecting, heading, and shooting. The book does not include drills to develop the special skills of goalkeepers. Instead, the book focuses on developing spatial, movement, and skill concepts for field players.

Chapters 1 through 6 include activities for individual, partner, small-, and large-group drill work. Many drills contain more than one performance level. The higher the level, the more difficult the drill. Factors influencing the difficulty of the drill will vary and may include the addition of players as defenders, changing spatial requirements, and combining movement with skills. Each drill is labeled according to its appropriateness: beginner (ages 5 and 6), advanced beginner (ages 7 and 8), intermediate (ages 9 and 10), and advanced (ages 11 and 12).

Chapter 6, "Game Progressions," discusses a plan for implementing structured games according to players' readiness. The chapter identifies the concepts that the coach can present at the 4 v 4, 5 v 5, 8 v 8, and 11 v 11 levels. Chapter 7, "Using Drills in Practice," offers information about practice organization and includes sample practice plans for 5- to 6-year-olds, 7- to 8-year-olds, 9- to 10-year-olds, and 11- to 12-year-olds.

A drill finder is included to help make the drills more user friendly. The drill finder lists the skills and concepts, highlighted by the level of defensive pressure and the number of players in each drill. To use the drill finder, coaches should select the skill or concept they are interested in from the left column. The column headings on top indicate the type of defensive pressure presented in the drill.

The headings on the bottom indicate the number of players in the drill. For example, a coach can look at the drill finder to locate a drill that would help improve dribbling skills for small groups, with no defensive pressure. The drill finder shows that drills 18 and 21 would meet these requirements.

Coaches using this book will find it a great benefit. They can help their players move more efficiently by using the drills that target direction, speed, and level. They will have a resource that guides them toward a logical order of teaching skills and concepts. They will improve safety and reduce collisions during practices and games by using the information about movement concepts. In addition, coaches will benefit by developing a better understanding of what concepts they should present at each age level.

The book is not all-inclusive. Coaches should feel free to substitute some of their favorite drills where appropriate in the progression.

Many of the activities included in this book are original ideas, while I collected some by observing other coaches, clinicians, and teaching professionals.

I encourage all coaches to have fun using this book. Your players will be grateful and will never have to say the sun went down before they got their turn.

Drill Finder

CONCEPTS	NO DEFENSE		
Dribbling	24	18, 21	17, 19, 20, 22
Passing and collecting	32, 33, 38, 40, 45, 46	34, 35, 36, 37, 39, 41, 42, 44	31, 36, 43, 58
Heading	61, 62	63, 64, 65	62
Shooting	68, 70, 71, 75	69, 72, 73, 74	83, 84
Space	62	1, 2	3, 4
Movement	8, 9, 10		5, 6, 7, 11, 13, 14
Number of players	**Single/partner**	**Small group**	**Large group**

CONCEPTS	SUBTLE DEFENSE		
Dribbling	24	23	29
Passing and collecting		47, 48, 49, 54	60
Heading		66	
Shooting	70, 71, 77	64, 65, 76, 78	
Space			
Movement			16
Number of players	**Single/partner**	**Small group**	**Large group**

CONCEPTS	GAMELIKE DEFENSE		
Dribbling	24, 25, 26, 27, 28		15, 30
Passing and collecting		50, 51, 53, 55, 57	52, 56, 59
Heading		67	
Shooting		76, 79	80, 81, 82
Space			
Movement	12		15
Number of players	**Single/partner**	**Small group**	**Large group**

1

Spatial Concepts and Movement Drills

The development of spatial and movement concepts should be an integral part of a beginning player's training. Often these concepts are neglected in favor of drills designed only for developing kicking, heading, and other ball skills. This neglect is unfortunate. Practice sessions must be more balanced to incorporate drills that help players develop spatial and movement skills. A player who understands spatial and movement concepts moves with confidence and incurs fewer injuries caused by collision.

Spatial concepts are essential for tactical awareness, which helps a player decide where or when to move to support a teammate who has the ball. Understanding spatial concepts also allows a player in possession of the ball to make better tactical decisions concerning where and when to penetrate the defense using dribbling, passing, and shooting skills. Spatial concepts deal with where to move on the field. Training in spatial concepts includes teaching concepts of open space, closed space, personal space, general space, and vision:

- Open space—space that is unoccupied by players
- Closed space—space that is occupied by one or more players
- Personal space—the space that immediately surrounds a player
- General space—the entire area in which a player is allowed to function
- Vision—the entire field of vision a player must monitor, using scanning techniques to improve peripheral vision

Movement concepts deal with how players negotiate space. The development of movement concepts includes training in direction, speed, and level:

- Direction—ability to maintain or change pathway
- Speed—ability to change rate of motion
- Level—position of a player's body in relation to the playing surface, such as in jumping (high level) or sliding (low level)

The drills presented in this chapter develop space and movement concepts progressively. They begin with demonstrations of open and closed space. These are the fundamental concepts that guide much of the process of deciding where to move and where to play the ball next. These demonstrations come first in the progression as a safety concern, to help reduce collisions.

Personal- and general-space demonstrations are second in the progression. These exercises help to achieve field balance and to avoid clustering of players. Visual training follows, although it is also intertwined with demonstrations of open, closed, personal, and general space. The visual-training drills develop awareness of good visual habits, such as breaking eye contact with the ground and scanning the periphery. These habits improve a player's range of vision on the field.

Next in the progression are elements of movement that help players to create or deny space. These elements include direction, speed, and level. Players can create space (move to open space away from other players) or deny space (move toward other players to close space) by changing directions, speeds, and levels more efficiently than their opponents do. All of the exercises are presented developmentally, gradually increasing the expectations for speed of execution.

Many of the drills do not initially use a ball. In this way, beginning players gain confidence in their moving skills without having to control a ball. As players demonstrate competence with movement, they can add a ball to increase the challenge.

1   OPEN-SPACE DEMONSTRATION

PURPOSE

To help players recognize how easy it is to move through unoccupied spaces. Use this demonstration to build a base of knowledge about the use of space, and refer to it in later teachings.

LEVEL

Beginner

EQUIPMENT

One ball, two game markers

TIME

5 minutes

PROCEDURE

Level 1

1. Players huddle in a group.
2. Place two markers on a line about 10 yards apart.
3. One player stands by one of the markers.
4. The same player walks to the other marker (see figure).

Level 2

1. Repeat procedures 1 and 2 from level 1.
2. One player stands by one of the markers with a ball.
3. The same player dribbles the ball to the other marker.

Level 3

1. Repeat procedures 1 and 2 from level 1.
2. One player stands by one of the markers with a ball, and another player stands by the other marker.
3. The player with the ball passes the ball to the teammate who is standing by the other marker.

1

KEY POINTS

You have demonstrated how uncomplicated it is to move, dribble, and pass through open space. Young players will develop a more thorough understanding of space when you give them a visual demonstration. Refer to this demonstration often when explaining effective use of space in training and game situations.

RELATED DRILL

2

10 yd

2 CLOSED-SPACE DEMONSTRATION

PURPOSE

To demonstrate how impossible it is to move, dribble, and pass through closed spaces.

LEVEL

Beginner

EQUIPMENT

Two game markers, one ball

TIME

5 minutes

PROCEDURE

Level 1

1. Players huddle in a group.
2. Place two markers on a line about 10 yards apart.
3. Player A stands by one of the markers.
4. Player B stands on the line at a point midway between the markers.
5. Player A walks on the line to the other marker.

Level 2

1. Repeat procedures 1 through 4 from level 1, except player A has a ball.
2. Player A dribbles the ball to the opposite marker without going off the line (see figure).

Level 3

1. Repeat procedures 1 through 4 from level 1, except player A has a ball.
2. Player C stands by the unoccupied marker.
3. Player A passes the ball to player C.

KEY POINTS

At level 1, player A will find this task impossible because player B, who has closed the space between the two markers, has blocked his pathway. At level 2, player A will not be able to dribble the ball through the space closed by player B. At level 3, player A will not be able to pass the ball through the space closed by player B.

Understanding open versus closed space should be a top priority for young players. Give them this visual demonstration of how impossible it is to move without the ball, to dribble with the ball, or to pass the ball through closed spaces. Refer to this demonstration when players begin clustering, colliding with teammates or opponents, or dribbling and passing into closed spaces. Explain to them the alternative—which is, of course, to use open space.

RELATED DRILL

1

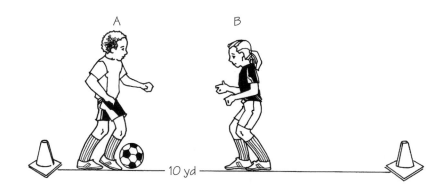

10 yd

PERSONAL-SPACE DEMONSTRATION

PURPOSE

To develop an understanding that personal space is the space that immediately surrounds each player, and that player movement affects it.

LEVEL

Beginner

EQUIPMENT

Nine game markers

TIME

5 minutes

PROCEDURE

1. Divide players into groups of five. Players form four grids, each of which measures 5 yards by 5 yards, with one group in each grid. Number the grids 1 through 4.
2. Players move freely within each grid (see figure).
3. If a player touches another player, they both are frozen
4. The players from grid 2 join the players from grid 1, and the players from grid 3 join the players from grid 4.
5. At this point, all frozen players become unfrozen and rejoin the other players.
6. Players move freely in their grids for about 30 seconds.
7. Finally, all of the players move to grid 1.
8. Players move freely for about 30 seconds (remind them not to touch anyone as they move).

KEY POINTS

As the players move in a grid with only four other players, maintaining their personal space should not be challenging. As the number of players in a space increases, movement becomes more difficult. When all the players are moving in a small space, it becomes almost impossible to maintain their personal space or not to invade someone else's. During scrimmages and games, this drill can serve as a visual reminder that movement becomes difficult when players cluster. The result should be better spacing and less swarming so that players can maintain their personal spaces.

RELATED DRILLS

1, 2, 4

4 GENERAL-SPACE DEMONSTRATION

PURPOSE

To develop an understanding that general space is the entire area in which a player can function and that within this general space, larger spaces are easier to negotiate than smaller ones.

LEVEL

Beginner

EQUIPMENT

Eight game markers

TIME

5 minutes

PROCEDURE

1. All players scatter within a grid identified by four game markers approximately 20 yards apart (see figure).
2. Players move freely through the entire grid.
3. Expand the size of the grid to 50 yards by 50 yards.
4. Players move freely through the larger grid.
5. After the players move in both grids, discuss with them in which grid they found it easier to move.

KEY POINTS

The personal-space demonstration showed how increasing the number of players in a space affected a player's personal space and movement. This drill demonstrates how increasing the size of the space makes player movement easier, because there is more time to make decisions about changing direction, speed, and level. Players should recognize that by using all the spaces within the general space properly, they maintain field balance and move more freely.

RELATED DRILLS

1, 2, 3

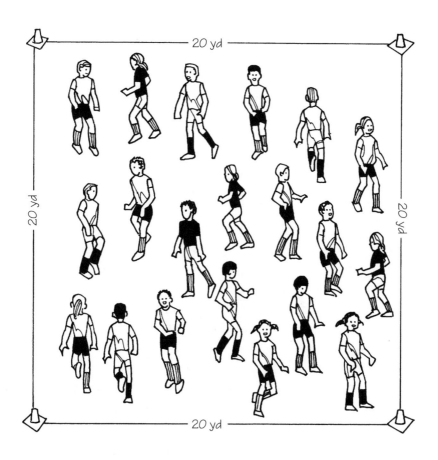

MOVING VISION DRILL

PURPOSE

To develop good visual habits when negotiating space with and without the ball.

LEVEL

Beginner

EQUIPMENT

One soccer ball for each player, four game markers

TIME

5 minutes

PROCEDURE

Level 1

1. Players scatter within a 30-yard by 30-yard grid (see figure).
2. On the coach's signal, players move freely throughout the grid by walking to a four-count rhythm.
3. Players take one step with the left foot, one step with the right, one step with the left again, looking left as they step, and one step with the right, looking right as they step.
4. Players verbalize the movement by chanting "left, right, look left, look right."
5. Players repeat the drill, this time while jogging.

Level 2

1. Repeat level 1 procedures while using a ball.

KEY POINTS

Movement affects a player's vision. You must train players to look constantly in the direction they are moving and to scan to right and left, so that they can negotiate space efficiently. Practice this visual drill before adding a ball. Adding a ball adversely affects vision. Beginning players, especially, like to look down at the ball to keep it under control. Insist that they look left and right during the sequence so that they break eye contact with the ball. If they seem out of control, ask them to slow down.

RELATED DRILLS

None

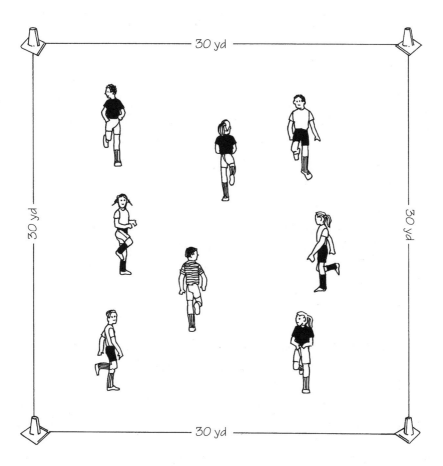

6   VOLCANO DRILL

PURPOSE

To develop an understanding of changing direction.

LEVEL

Beginner

EQUIPMENT

Four game markers plus one game marker for each player

TIME

5 minutes

PROCEDURE

1. Players scatter throughout a 20-yard by 20-yard grid.
2. Within the grid, scatter approximately sixteen markers, or one for each player. Players will pretend these markers are volcanoes (see figure).
3. On the coach's signal, players move through the grid.
4. As the players approach a volcano, they must quickly change directions to avoid being burned by any lava.
5. Challenge the players to see how many volcanoes they can pass in 30 seconds.

KEY POINTS

This drill will help players understand feinting. Demonstrate that to change directions quickly, players should flex one leg slightly and quickly push off the inside of the same foot. Encourage players to exaggerate this pushoff in a lateral direction. Players can apply more force in this lateral direction by flexing the leg. Incorporate different body parts (including the head, shoulders, and arms) in this shifting of weight from one direction to another. Have players experiment with combinations of feints—for example, feint right, left, then quickly back to the right.

RELATED DRILLS

7, 8

6

7   ZIGZAG DRILL

PURPOSE

To develop an understanding of changing directions.

LEVEL

Beginner

EQUIPMENT

Sixteen markers—four yellow, twelve green, twelve red

TIME

5 minutes

PROCEDURE

1. Make a 20-yard by 20-yard grid, using yellow markers to identify the corners.
2. Place green and red markers in three rows in random order (for example, green, red, green, red, red, green, green, red).
3. Be sure that each row has a different order.
4. Divide players equally behind the rows (see figure).
5. Players move down each row, negotiating the markers. If it is a green marker, they must feint to the right and continue to the next marker. If it is a red marker, they must feint to the left.
6. After players finish row one, they move to row two and then to row three. Row three players move to row one.
7. Repeat several times.

KEY POINTS

This drill encourages players to develop feinting moves, both left and right. Often players want to feint only to their dominant side. Encourage players to exaggerate movement using quick bursts of energy in lateral directions.

RELATED DRILLS

6, 8

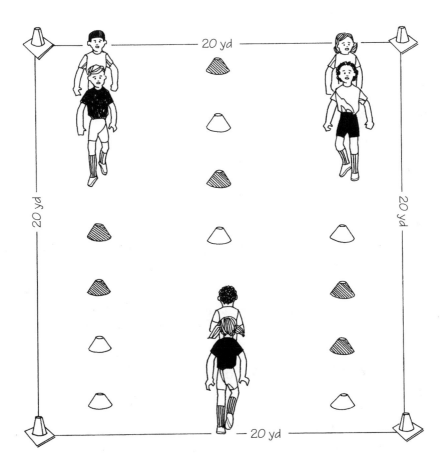

8   TRIANGLE DRILL

PURPOSE

To assess how well players are able to change direction and speed.

LEVEL

Beginner

EQUIPMENT

Three game markers

TIME

30 minutes

PROCEDURE

1. Place three game markers 10 feet apart in a triangle formation (see figure).
2. On the coach's signal, players move laterally to touch one game marker, pivot, move laterally to the next marker, pivot again, and then move laterally to the third marker.
3. Players repeat this action for 30 seconds.
4. Players count the number of markers touched.

KEY POINTS

Use this simple drill to assess players' performance of lateral movements and of changes in direction and speed. Adding the pivot enables players to develop the change of direction skills that will often be required in game situations. You should not compare players' results. The purpose of this drill is not to determine which player performs the best, but simply to show players their individual improvement.

RELATED DRILLS

10, 11, 12

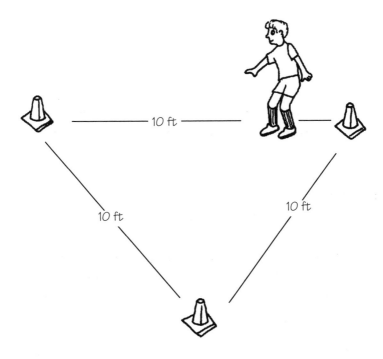

10 ft

10 ft

10 ft

PURPOSE

To demonstrate how changing speed creates space.

LEVEL

Beginner

EQUIPMENT

Four game markers for every two players

TIME

5 minutes

PROCEDURE

1. Place two players in a 10-yard by 10-yard grid.
2. Player B stands behind player A on the side of the grid (see figure).
3. Player A moves to the opposite side of the grid by jogging at a constant speed.
4. Player B follows player A, maintaining an arm's-length distance.
5. Player A moves to the opposite side of the grid again, but this time by changing speeds—accelerating quickly, slowly, more slowly, more quickly—in a herky-jerky fashion.
6. Players reverse roles several times during the drill.

KEY POINTS

Players should recognize that when they move at the same pace the opponent can easily defend against them, assuming both players are of equal athletic ability. In this drill, if a player moves at a constant pace, it should not be difficult to maintain an arm's-length distance. However, if a player changes speeds quickly, defending—or in this case, maintaining an arm's-length distance—becomes very difficult.

RELATED DRILLS

12, 13, 14

10   COPYCAT DRILL

PURPOSE
To demonstrate how changing speed and direction creates space.

LEVEL
Beginner

EQUIPMENT
Four game markers

TIME
5 minutes

PROCEDURE
1. Two players stand side by side on a line of a 20-yard by 20-yard grid (see figure).
2. On the coach's signal, player A begins to move forward, changing speeds as she goes.
3. Player B looks at player A and copies her movements.
4. If player A comes to a stop, she can reverse directions and go back toward the line where she started, again changing speeds.
5. Player A may choose to change speeds and directions several times.
6. When the coach signals to stop, player B should still be beside player A.
7. Reverse roles several times during the drill.

KEY POINTS
Coaches should encourage players to use short bursts of speed and changes of direction to create space between themselves and their opponents.

RELATED DRILLS
9, 11

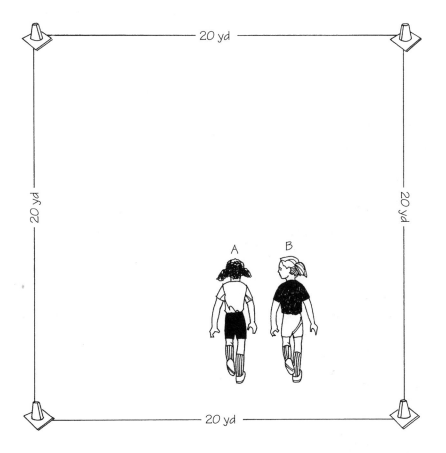

11 MONDAY MORNING TRAFFIC DRILL

PURPOSE

To demonstrate how changing speed and direction creates space.

LEVEL

Beginner

EQUIPMENT

Four game markers

TIME

5 minutes

PROCEDURE

1. Scatter players with partners in a 15-yard by 15-yard grid.
2. Player B will be the driver of the car. Player A is the backseat passenger whom player B is driving to work (see figure).
3. Player B moves through the grid, changing speeds and directions and avoiding other drivers who are also on their way to work.
4. The backseat passengers are responsible for following their drivers closely, always maintaining an arm's-length distance from them.
5. Reverse roles several times during the drill.

KEY POINTS

This drill can be equivalent to typical Monday morning traffic during rush hour, including traffic jams and fender benders. Coaches should encourage all players to change speed and direction—and monitor the movements of other pairs—to avoid collisions.

RELATED DRILLS

9, 10, 12

FLAG TAG

PURPOSE

To demonstrate how changing speed and direction creates space.

LEVEL

Beginner

EQUIPMENT

Four game markers for every two players, one flag belt for each player

TIME

5 minutes

PROCEDURE

Level 1

1. Position two players at opposite sides of a 10-yard by 10-yard grid (see figure).
2. Players wear flag belts.
3. On the coach's signal, player A approaches player B and tries to pull one of her flags.
4. Player B tries to change speed and direction to get to the opposite side of the grid without having a flag pulled.
5. Player A will earn 1 point if he can grab the flag.
6. If player B can get to the opposite side of the grid, she earns 1 point.
7. The player who earns 5 points first is the winner.
8. Players then reverse roles.

Level 2

1. Place six players, two teams of three each, in a 20-yard by 20-yard grid.
2. On the coach's signal, players try to steal the opposite team's flags.
3. A player whose flag is pulled must wait to partner up with a teammate before again helping to grab flags.

4. The team that captures all the other team's flags first is the winner.

KEY POINTS

Encourage player A to close the space toward player B by making a bending run at her and by assuming a good defensive stance. A bending run means the defender approaches his opponent using a curved pathway instead of a straight line. A curved pathway allows the defender to guide the opponent toward a part of the square that reduces the amount of territory to defend (for example, toward a teammate or a boundary line). Spacing of players is important at level 2.

RELATED DRILLS

9, 10, 11

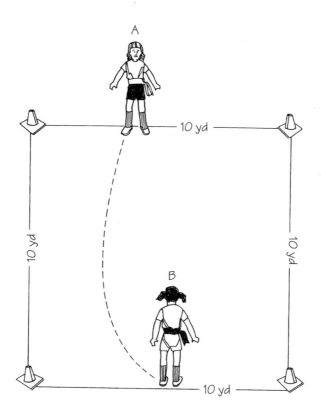

PURPOSE

To demonstrate how to change speeds and directions to avoid closed spaces.

LEVEL

Beginner

EQUIPMENT

Four game markers

TIME

5 minutes

PROCEDURE

1. Divide players into four equal groups. Position one group on each side of a 10-yard by 10-yard grid (see figure).
2. On the coach's signal, players exchange places with the group opposite them.
3. Vary the movement by walking, jogging, and running.

KEY POINTS

All players will be moving to get to the opposite side of the grid. Changing speeds with the adjacent group will be essential to avoid closed spaces. This drill is more gamelike because it simulates the challenge of movement during games. Many times teammates and opponents will be clustered while moving in opposite directions toward each other. Other times, teammates and opponents will cross pathways with each other. Avoiding collision by changing speed and direction will reduce the possibility of injury.

RELATED DRILL

15

10 yd

10 yd

10 yd

10 yd

14 JACKRABBIT DRILL

PURPOSE

To develop balance while changing levels.

LEVEL

Beginner

EQUIPMENT

Four game markers to identify grid, plus one game marker per player for inside grid

TIME

10 minutes

PROCEDURE

1. Scatter game markers in a 20-yard by 20-yard grid.
2. On the coach's signal, players move freely through the grid (see figure).
3. As they approach a marker, players jump with two feet as high as they can over the marker, landing lightly on two feet. As they land, they quickly change direction.
4. After repeating this action several times, players jump, taking off with one foot and landing on both feet.
5. Players jump again, this time taking off with two feet and landing on the left foot; they push off and change direction to the right.
6. Players repeat this action and then switch, landing on the right foot and changing direction to the left.

KEY POINTS

Encourage players to use their arms to generate momentum when they jump and to aid balance when they land.

RELATED DRILLS

None

15 **SHIRT TAG**

PURPOSE

To develop an understanding of direction, speed, and level, and their relationship to movement.

LEVEL

Beginner

EQUIPMENT

One scrimmage jersey for each player, four game markers, several balls

TIME

8 to 10 minutes

PROCEDURE

Level 1

1. Players scatter in a 20-yard by 20-yard grid.
2. Each player has a jersey tucked into the back of his pants (see figure).
3. On the coach's signal, players travel through the grid, trying to grab the tucked scrimmage jersey of another player.
4. Players try to grab as many shirts as possible in a two-minute period.
5. If a player's jersey is pulled, he must go outside the grid and do 10 touches on a ball before returning to the game. At the end of two minutes, stop and give all players a chance to get ready for a new game.

Level 2

1. Repeat level 1, procedures 1 and 2.
2. Each player moves through the grid with a ball while trying to collect jerseys.

KEY POINTS

Encourage players to avoid closed spaces as they change directions, speeds, and levels. Change the specific skill that eliminated players must execute for each game, for example, 10 rollovers, 8 stepovers, and so forth. For variety, divide group into two teams and play team shirt tag. When playing shirt tag level 2, players who lose control of their balls while trying to collect a jersey must go outside the grid.

RELATED DRILL

19

20 yd

20 yd

20 yd

20 yd

NUMBER TAG

PURPOSE

To develop an understanding of direction, speed, and level, and of their relationships to movement.

LEVEL

Beginner

EQUIPMENT

Four game markers, a ball for each player (Level 2)

TIME

8 to 10 minutes

PROCEDURE

Level 1

1. All players line up on one side of a 30-yard by 30-yard grid.
2. Each player has a number from 1 to 4.
3. Two players (defenders) stand between the line of players and the opposite line, which is safe territory (see figure).
4. Defenders call a number.
5. The player whose number they call tries to travel through open space to the safe line.
6. A player who is tagged must sit down.
7. When the next number is called, that player can try to free the players sitting down by touching them while on the way to safe territory.
8. A player who is freed must try to get to the safe zone without being tagged.

Level 2

1. Repeat level 1 procedures, except players on the line must reach the safety zone while dribbling a ball.
2. A player whose ball is touched by a defender must sit down.

KEY POINTS

Coaches should encourage players to be in control as they change direction, speed, and level. Defenders should make bending runs as they try to capture players, and should avoid having two defenders chase one player (unless he is the only one left). During level 2 action, encourage numbered players to shield the ball from defenders while traveling toward the safety zone.

RELATED DRILL

15

Safe territory
30 yd

2

Dribbling Drills

Players who successfully master spatial and movement concepts are able to travel through space efficiently. Using these concepts when in possession of the ball, however, requires devoting time to improving ball skills. Players can work on these skills in formal practice sessions and in informal sessions at home. The drills presented in this chapter will help to develop one of these ball skills—dribbling. Dribbling means applying controlled touches to the ball, using various surfaces of the foot, so that the ball remains within playing distance of the dribbler. It is one of the ways to advance the ball through open space or to create open spaces when a player is tightly defended against. Players can dribble in a straight line, using the inside or outside of the foot, when moving through open space.

Negotiating closed spaces requires changing the position of the ball in relation to the body as well as changing the position of the body in relation to the ball (feinting). The following are examples of changing the position of the ball in relation to the body:

- Pushaway—using a surface of the foot to quickly move the ball away from the body and stop it
- Pullback—using a surface of the foot, usually the sole, to bring the ball back toward the body and stop it
- Rollover—using a surface of the foot on the ball to roll the ball forward, backward, or sideways

The following dribbling moves are examples of changing the position of the body in relation to the ball:

- Stepover—stepping over the ball to its left with the right foot and pivoting back to right on the right foot (also done with left foot going to the right of the ball and pivoting back to left)
- Scissors—stepping over the ball, feinting left, and touching ball to right with outside of right foot (also done with opposite feinting action)
- Walkover—simply walking over the ball and turning

The dribbling drills in this chapter progress from least to most difficult. They include

1. stationary dribbling activities,
2. dribbling and movement with no defensive pressure,
3. dribbling with subtle defensive pressure, and
4. dribbling with gamelike defensive pressure.

Performing a skill from a stationary position is simpler than performing it while moving. When a player is stationary, her visual focus is not affected by negotiating space with other players. Therefore, a player can devote all of her visual attention to the skill, not to how and where to move. After players gain some confidence with dribbling skills from a stationary position, challenge them by placing them in motion—without the added burden of defensive pressure. This will allow them the time and space needed to develop these skills. As they become more competent with dribbling, add defensive pressure. The degree of difficulty increases; players cannot just focus on the technical aspects of dribbling (the "how to"), but must also concentrate on tactical elements (the "when" and "where"). There should be a gradual increase from subtle to gamelike pressure. Give players opportunities to practice penetrating dribbling skills, since the role of the first attacker (the player with the ball) is to penetrate the defense. Small-sided drills provide such opportunities during practice sessions.

When using these drills, exercise patience and allow players to progress from a slow, methodical pace to a more gamelike pace. Expecting players to perform new moves under pressure before they are ready will lead to frustration and failure and may cause them to abandon any effort to master new moves. Allow players to improve at their own rates.

Improved dribbling skills will enable players to keep the ball longer, penetrate the defense, create spaces for passing and shooting, and relieve defensive pressure.

17   FANCY FOOTWORK DRILL

PURPOSE

To improve ability to control the ball while in a stationary position, with no defensive pressure.

LEVEL

Beginner, advanced beginner

EQUIPMENT

One soccer ball for each player, four game markers

TIME

10 to 15 minutes

PROCEDURE

1. Players (with balls) scatter in a 20-yard by 20-yard grid (see figure).
2. While stationary, players practice controlled touches on the ball.
3. Players can combine these touches in various ways to change speed, direction, or level. Encourage players to change the position of the ball in relation to the body with pushaways, pullbacks, rollovers, and so forth.
4. Players then practice changing body position in relation to the ball with stepovers, scissors, walkovers, and so forth.

KEY POINTS

There should be time for hundreds of touches on the ball during each practice. Encourage players to explore ways to move the ball using the inside, outside, sole, and heel of each foot. Players may mirror individual moves demonstrated by coaches, but encourage them to create new combinations of moves. As they touch the ball, encourage them to maintain good vision constantly. For variety, and to reduce fatigue, use partners. Have one partner work on skills for a minute and then give the ball to the other partner. Repeat. Change formations using triangles, circles, and so forth to add variety to this drill. Give players time to develop these skills from a stationary position, without movement into other spaces and without defensive pressure. Players should practice these moves at home as part of a daily routine.

RELATED DRILLS

None

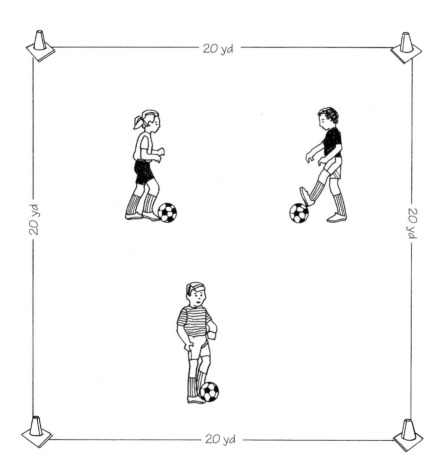

18   FOLLOW THE LEADER DRILL

PURPOSE

To develop dribbling skills while negotiating space with no defensive pressure.

LEVEL

Beginner, advanced beginner, intermediate

EQUIPMENT

One soccer ball for each player, four game markers

TIME

5 minutes

PROCEDURE

1. Players divide into lines of four or five players, in a 20-yard by 20-yard grid (see figure).
2. The first player in line is the leader and begins moving through the grid. The rest of the players follow while dribbling their balls.
3. On the coach's signal, the last person in line pushes his ball out approximately 5 yards in front of the leader, sprints after it, and becomes the new leader.
4. The new last person repeats this action on the next whistle.

KEY POINTS

Encourage ball control by discussing the force exerted on the ball when various parts of the foot are used to touch it. Review the proper use of the general space provided so that lines of players don't move into the same space. As players achieve greater control over their movements, allow players to do this drill without the coach's signals.

RELATED DRILLS

19, 20, 21

19 FREEDOM DRILL

PURPOSE

To develop dribbling skills while negotiating space with no defensive pressure.

LEVEL

Advanced beginner

EQUIPMENT

One soccer ball for every two players, five game markers

TIME

8 to 10 minutes

PROCEDURE

1. Partners space themselves around a circle approximately 30 yards in diameter (see figure).
2. On the coach's whistle, the partner with the ball travels into the circle, practicing her individual moves as she encounters other players who are doing likewise.
3. After a minute of moving, the player with the ball returns and gives the ball to her partner, who repeats the action.
4. Players have complete freedom to use any of their individual moves during this drill.

KEY POINTS

Encourage players to use a variety of individual moves to change directions, speeds, and levels as they negotiate space. Refer to the demonstration on spatial and movement concepts if players are moving into closed spaces. This drill is the next step in the dribbling progression, because it requires using individual moves to travel through the space provided. The drill allows players the freedom to develop skills without defensive pressure.

RELATED DRILLS

18, 20, 21

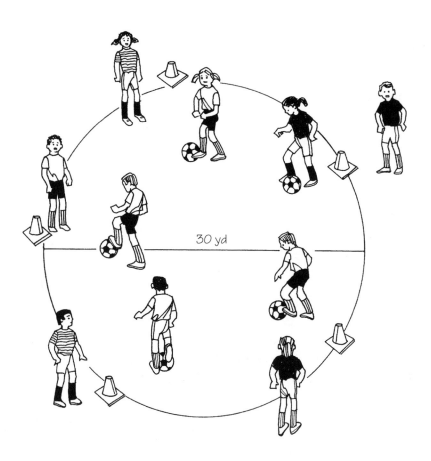

30 yd

20 FREEZE DRILL

PURPOSE

To develop dribbling skills while negotiating space with no defensive pressure.

LEVEL

Advanced beginner

EQUIPMENT

One soccer ball for each player, four game markers

TIME

7 to 10 minutes

PROCEDURE

1. Players scatter in a 20-yard by 20-yard grid.
2. All players move freely through the grid with a ball (see figure).
3. When the coach signals by blowing a whistle, the players must freeze by bringing their balls to a complete stop.
4. Variations of this drill might include touching the ball with any body part on one side of the body, freezing on a specific number of body parts, or freezing at various levels.

KEY POINTS

This drill allows players to develop individual moves while negotiating space without defensive pressure. Encourage players to use body parts on their nondominant side. Freezing at various levels might include straight-legged, crouching, or kneeling positions.

RELATED DRILLS

18, 19, 21

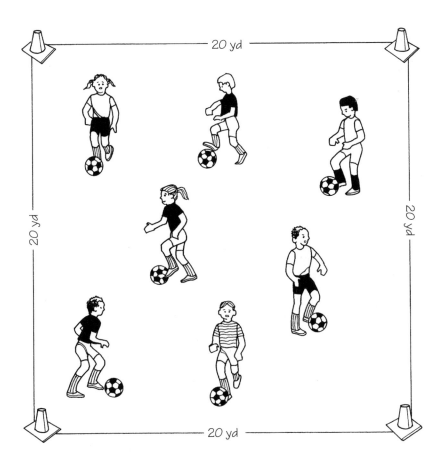

20 yd

20 yd

20 yd

20 yd

21 PARTNER TAG

PURPOSE

To develop dribbling skills while negotiating space with no defensive pressure.

LEVEL

Beginner, advanced beginner

EQUIPMENT

One soccer ball for every two players, four game markers

TIME

7 to 10 minutes

PROCEDURE

1. In a 20-yard-by-20-yard grid, each player chooses a partner and holds hands with her.
2. One set of partners has a ball. The rest of the balls are outside the grid (see figure).
3. On the coach's signal, the pair with the ball acts as a chaser and moves through the grid dribbling the ball, until they get close enough to another pair to pass the ball and hit them.
4. If the ball hits a set of partners, they must get a ball from outside the grid and become another pair of chasers.
5. The game continues until there is only one pair left who aren't chasers.

KEY POINTS

This is a fun game that requires partners to coordinate their movements. Emphasize passing to hit other pairs, not to shoot hard at them.

RELATED DRILLS

18, 19, 20

SPRINT DRILL

PURPOSE

To develop dribbling skills and speed for negotiating space, with no defensive pressure.

LEVEL

Intermediate, advanced

EQUIPMENT

One soccer ball for each player, four game markers

TIME

5 minutes

PROCEDURE

1. Players scatter in a 20-yard by 20-yard grid, each with a ball.
2. The players travel through the grid until they hear the coach's whistle.
3. On that signal, players dribble their balls as fast as they can out of the grid (see figure).
4. They continue dribbling as fast as they can until they hear a second whistle.
5. Then the players dribble as fast as they can back to the grid, where they continue to travel through the grid at a moderate pace.

KEY POINTS

Present this drill only when players have developed sufficient ball control skills. Encourage them to push the ball away to open spaces at a distance of 5 to 7 yards, then sprint to the ball. Kicking the ball as far as they can and sprinting after it is not the purpose of this drill. After players become more highly skilled with speed dribbling, add players in the grid without a ball. On the coach's signal, the players without a ball chase the players who are speed dribbling.

RELATED DRILL

25

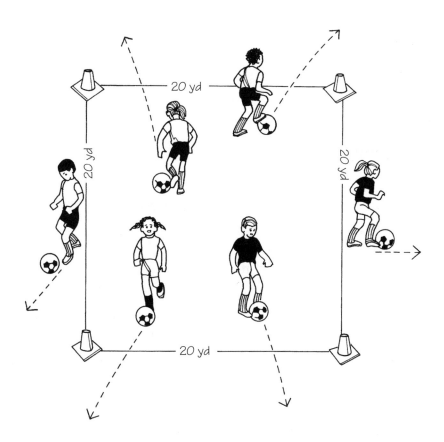

23

PURPOSE

To develop dribbling skills with subtle defensive pressure.

LEVEL

Advanced beginner, intermediate

EQUIPMENT

Two soccer balls and four game markers for every six players

TIME

8 to 10 minutes

PROCEDURE

Level 1

1. Place six players in a 10-yard by 10-yard grid.
2. Four players form a circle.
3. Two players, each with a ball, stand outside the circle on opposite sides (see figure).
4. Designate one of these players as the tagger.
5. On the coach's signal, the tagger has 30 seconds to catch the other player with a ball, while both players are dribbling.
6. The tagger may cut through the circle, but the player being chased may not.

Level 2

1. Repeat level 1, procedures 1 through 6.
2. While the tagger is chasing the other player, teammates who have formed the circle move as a unit to shield the player being chased from the tagger.

KEY POINTS

Players need to use good visual habits to know when the tagger has changed directions. Changing directions and speeds frequently will help the player being chased.

RELATED DRILLS

None

24

SHAKE-AND-TAKE DRILL

PURPOSE

To develop dribbling skills used to create space and go to the goal (under defensive pressure in levels 2 and 3).

LEVEL

Advanced beginner, intermediate, advanced

EQUIPMENT

One soccer ball for each player, one marker for each goal, four goals

TIME

10 minutes

PROCEDURE

Level 1

1. Place a marker 40 yards from the goal.
2. A player dribbles toward the marker, executes an individual move to create space (a scissors move, for example), and then goes to the goal and shoots (see figure).

Level 2

1. Place two markers 40 yards from the goal, about 5 yards apart.
2. A defender stands on a line between the markers and tries to tackle the ball away from the attacker, as the attacker attempts to go between the markers to the goal.

Level 3

1. Player A stands 40 yards from the goal.
2. A defender stands 30 yards from the goal.
3. The ball is passed to player A.
4. When player A touches the ball, the defender may pursue him.
5. Player A uses individual moves to create space to go to the goal.

SHAKE-AND-TAKE DRILL

KEY POINTS

Allow players to develop individual moves with imaginary pressure (the marker in level 1) until they experience success. When their skills have improved to the point at which they need more challenge, add a defender who can only move laterally (level 2). This change will add subtle pressure. A defender applies gamelike pressure at level 3. Do not rush players through their progressions. Use as many goals as are available, or make temporary goals, so players have many opportunities.

RELATED DRILLS

27, 28

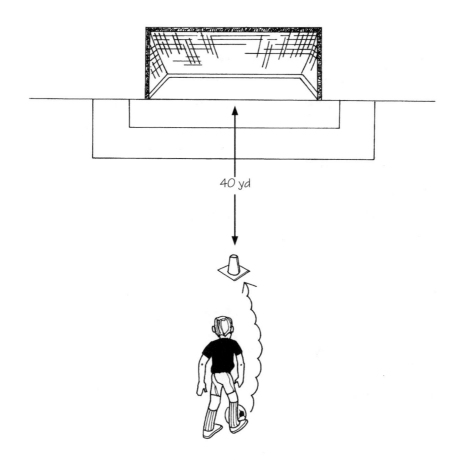

40 yd

SPRINT CHALLENGE DRILL

PURPOSE

To develop dribbling skills and speed when confronted with game-like defensive pressure.

LEVEL

Intermediate, advanced

EQUIPMENT

One soccer ball for every three players, four goals

TIME

10 minutes

PROCEDURE

Level 1

1. Player A stands about 5 yards behind player B.
2. The coach passes the ball forward.
3. Player B must collect the ball, sprint toward the goal, and shoot before the defender, player A, can catch him.
4. Variations include serving balls at various speeds, directions, and levels.

Level 2

1. Repeat level 1, procedures 1 through 4.
2. Repeat the action, but add a goalkeeper to increase the defensive pressure (see figure).

KEY POINTS

Encourage players to push the ball out 5 to 7 yards to maintain both speed and control. When adding a goalkeeper, restrict him by not allowing him to come off the goal line. As skills increase, add more goalkeeping pressure.

RELATED DRILLS

22

Coach

B

A

POSSESSION DRILL

PURPOSE

To develop shielding and dribbling techniques under gamelike pressure.

LEVEL

Beginner, intermediate, advanced

EQUIPMENT

One soccer ball, four game markers

TIME

5 minutes

PROCEDURE

1. Position four game markers to make a 10-yard by 10-yard grid.
2. Position two players inside the grid, one with the ball and the other as a defender (see figure).
3. On the coach's signal, the player with the ball combines shielding and dribbling techniques to keep possession of the ball for 30 seconds.
4. After 30 seconds, reverse roles.

KEY POINTS

A key element to success for any team involved in a game such as soccer is to keep possession of the ball. A team retains possession partly because individual team members know how to shield and dribble to create spaces for penetrating the defense. Penetration is the role of the first attacker. The first attacker is defined as the player with the ball. During this drill, encourage offensive players to keep their bodies between the ball and the defender. When shielding, insist they try to position themselves "sideways on" to the defender. This position allows them to have the greatest distance between the defender and the ball.

RELATED DRILL

27

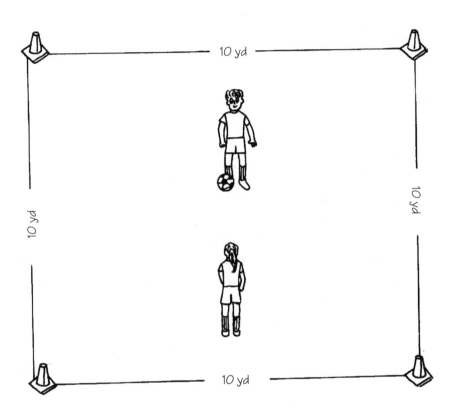

27   PARTNER DRIBBLE GAME

PURPOSE

To develop dribbling skills to create space under gamelike defensive pressure.

LEVEL

Advanced beginner, intermediate, advanced

EQUIPMENT

One soccer ball and four game markers for every two players

TIME

8 to 10 minutes

PROCEDURE

1. In a 10-yard by 10-yard grid, one partner stands on a line with a ball and the other partner stands on the opposite side of the square (see figure).
2. Player A passes the ball to player B.
3. When player B receives the ball, player A pursues her in an effort to close her space and touch the ball, or to force her out of the grid.
4. If player A touches the ball, she earns 1 point.
5. If player B can dribble safely to the opposite line, she earns 2 points.
6. The first player to earn 6 points is the winner.
7. Then they reverse roles.

KEY POINTS

The offensive player in this drill earns more points for being successful because this is an offensive drill. Encourage the offensive player to use a variety of moves to create space.

RELATED DRILLS

24, 28

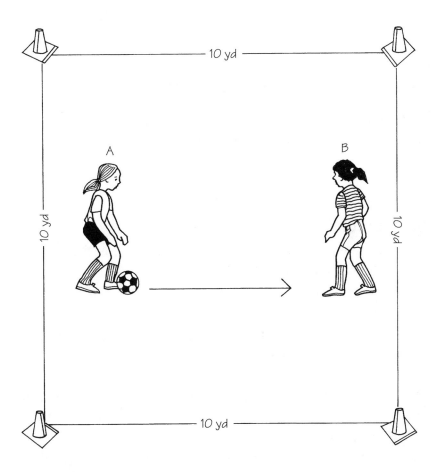

28 DRIBBLE BASEBALL GAME

PURPOSE

To develop dribbling skills to create space under gamelike defensive pressure.

LEVEL

Advanced beginner, intermediate

EQUIPMENT

One soccer ball and eight game markers for every two players

TIME

10 to 12 minutes

PROCEDURE

1. Set up markers approximately 40 feet apart, in the shape of a baseball diamond (see figure).
2. Player B passes the ball to player A, who is positioned at home base.
3. When player A touches the ball, player B can pursue her.
4. Player A can choose to dribble through any of the markers.
5. If she dribbles through the markers at first base, she receives 1 point; second base, 2 points; third base, 3 points.
6. If player A can go through any of the markers and return home before player B touches the ball, she earns 4 points for a home run.
7. Player B, the defender, can earn an out by touching the ball.
8. After three outs, the players switch roles.

KEY POINTS

Encourage players to use their individual moves creatively to change direction. If defenders are having difficulty getting outs, set a run limit. If players are having trouble scoring runs, widen the markers that form the bases.

RELATED DRILLS

24, 27

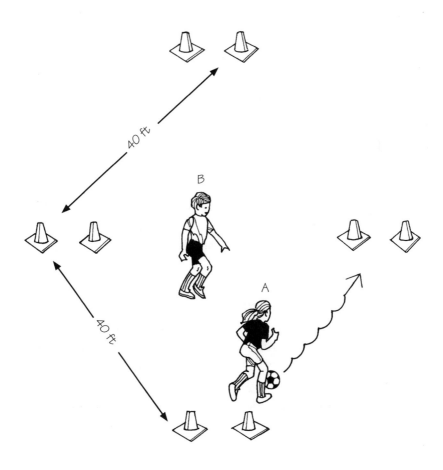

29 FOUR-GRID SCRAMBLE DRILL

PURPOSE

To develop dribbling techniques and tactics while negotiating space under subtle defensive pressure.

LEVEL

Intermediate, advanced

EQUIPMENT

Twelve soccer balls, sixteen game markers

TIME

10 minutes

PROCEDURE

1. Position game markers to make four 20-yard by 20-yard grids.
2. Place four players in each grid, three with a ball, one without (see figure).
3. On the coach's signal, the player without the ball chases the other players in an attempt to touch a ball.
4. If the player without a ball touches another player's ball or causes a player to dribble his ball out of the grid, the ball becomes the possession of the player without the ball.
5. The new player without a ball must then chase another player to gain possession of a ball, but may not regain possession from the player who caused him to lose possession.

KEY POINTS

This drill offers hundreds of touches and maximum activity while developing the technical aspect of the first attacker's dribbling skills. Using four grids with four players (instead of one large grid with sixteen players) enables them to concentrate on dribbling skills, without the visual distraction of numerous players. Using a defender to provide subtle defensive pressure adds tactical decision-making to the task. To challenge more highly skilled players, reduce the size of the grid (so players can develop dribbling skills in tight spaces) or add a second defender (player without a ball). If you add a second defender, increase the number of players in the grid to five.

RELATED DRILLS

27, 28, 30

PURPOSE

To develop dribbling techniques and tactics under gamelike defensive pressure.

LEVEL

Intermediate, advanced

EQUIPMENT

Three soccer balls, twelve game markers, six red and six blue jerseys

TIME

10 minutes

PROCEDURE

1. Position three pairs of game markers in a line, 20 yards apart, to make three 2-yard-wide goals.

2. On the opposite side of the field, 40 yards from the first line of markers, position three other sets in a line, 20 yards apart, to make three other 2-yard-wide goals (see figure).

3. In the middle of the field, position three red and three blue players.

4. Position one blue player 5 yards behind each blue goal and one red player 5 yards behind each red goal. These players are not goalies. They restart the action after each score.

5. On the coach's signal, players from each team try to dribble through any of their opponent's goals, scoring 1 point for each successful attempt. The ball must be dribbled and not passed through the goal.

6. After each score the offensive player becomes a defender, and the defender becomes the new offensive player. The server behind the goal puts the ball in play, passing it to the new offensive player.

7. Play continues for 5 minutes, at which time the players in the middle switch roles with the servers.

8. The team with the most points after 10 minutes is the winner.

KEY POINTS

The role of the first attacker (player with the ball) is to penetrate
the defense. This drill provides players opportunities to develop
technical aspects of dribbling through lots of touches on the ball, as
well as opportunities for tactical (decision-making) development.
By allowing players to dribble through any of the opponents' three
goals instead of just one, this drill encourages lots of changes of direction with the ball. To add some variety, have the servers restart
play with throw-ins.

RELATED DRILLS

27, 28, 29

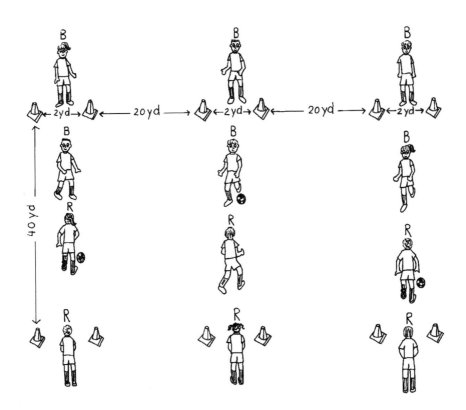

3

Passing and Collecting Drills

One of the most difficult tasks coaches have is developing their players' ability to connect consecutive passes. To acquire this ability, players must develop efficient passing and collecting techniques (how) and tactical knowledge (when and where). Collecting is the ability to gather in and control the ball using various parts of the body. Technical passing skills may be introduced as early as the beginner stage but should be more heavily emphasized in the other stages of development (advanced beginner, intermediate, advanced). Tactical knowledge generally increases with experience. Give players opportunities through small-sided drills to learn to pass through open spaces instead of spaces closed by defenders. They can also learn when it is appropriate to pass the ball to a teammate's feet and when they should play the ball through space to connect with a teammate making a run. Knowing which teammate to pass to is also important. Players should make passing choices in this order:

1. Pass to a teammate who is in position to score.
2. Pass to penetrate the defense and advance the ball in a forward direction.
3. Pass to a teammate who can relieve defensive pressure so that the offensive team can retain possession of the ball.

Passing choices may be limited by a player's physical ability, skill level, and field position, or even by the quality of the opponent. Passing choices increase when players move off the ball, improve skill level, take risks, and maintain good field vision.

This chapter presents drills in a progression:

1. Stationary passes to stationary target
2. Stationary passes to moving target
3. Moving passes to stationary target
4. Moving passes to moving target
5. Passing skills with subtle pressure
6. Passing skills with gamelike pressure

The drills emphasize the development of short-passing techniques. Encourage players to develop short-passing techniques that will allow them to deliver accurate, crisp, flat passes. Instruct players to rotate the heel of the kicking foot toward the target in a locked position, allowing the large inside surface of the foot to contact the ball. The foot should contact the upper half of the ball, which provides topspin on the ball and makes it stay low (flat) to the ground. Encourage players to exaggerate their follow-through with a high knee lift of the kicking leg. In the first stage of this progression, players learn how hard or softly they must kick a ball for it to travel a certain distance. Players will learn to judge leg speed and not to kick the ball with the same force regardless of the situation.

The first stage of the passing progression requires a stationary player to pass to a stationary target. These drills develop proper passing techniques by excluding performance inhibitors such as motion and defensive pressure.

When players have improved their passing techniques, challenge them by adding motion. Begin with the player passing to a moving target. This will require players to understand the relationships between the speed of the target player, the distance of the target, and the speed and angle of the pass. This scenario becomes more challenging in the next phase of the progression, as you put the passers in motion. Now they must compute all the factors involved in passing to a moving target, while negotiating space themselves. Beginning players may find this a visual nightmare. To limit frustration have players proceed slowly at first, gradually increasing their speed.

The final stage of the progression adds defensive pressure, which reduces time and space for making decisions. Progress from subtle to gamelike defensive pressure according to the players' ability.

As the players become more competent with passing skills, the quality of their play should improve. They should begin using soccer terminology that refers to the direction of the pass:

- Through pass—a pass that splits two defenders
- Square pass—a pass played to another player laterally (to the side)
- Back pass—a pass played in a backward direction, often referred to as a drop

With good communication and improved passing skills, your players' style of play will change from an individualistic, do-it-yourself style in which they always want to dribble, to one that is more team oriented and intentional in design.

PURPOSE

To develop an understanding of the application of force when passing the ball.

LEVEL

Beginner

EQUIPMENT

One soccer ball for every two players

TIME

5 to 7 minutes

PROCEDURE

1. Players stand approximately 5 yards from the sideline (see figure).
2. Players kick the ball so that it stops on the line.
3. Repeat several times.
4. Players repeat this action from 10-, 20-, and 30-yard distances.
5. Use partners to retrieve balls.

KEY POINTS

Discuss the proportional relationship between leg speed and the distance the ball travels. Encourage players to use proper kicking technique for making flat passes.

RELATED DRILLS

None

sideline

32 PARTNER PASSING DRILL

PURPOSE

To develop passing accuracy and collection skills from a stationary passer to a stationary target with no defensive pressure.

LEVEL

Beginner, advanced beginner

EQUIPMENT

One soccer ball for every two players, four game markers

TIME

8 to 10 minutes

PROCEDURE

Level 1

1. Players scatter within a 30-yard by 30-yard grid.
2. Partners should be about 10 yards apart.
3. Players pass to their partners, who will collect the balls and return the passes (see figure).
4. Encourage players to speak aloud the sequence of "collect, look, look right, and pass."
5. Players repeat the sequence, this time looking left, or looking left and right, before returning the pass.

Level 2

1. Repeat level 1, procedures 1 through 5.
2. Vary this activity by using three players in a triangle or several players in a circle formation.
3. After a stationary player passes to a stationary target, she may run to that player's space.

KEY POINTS

Beginning players should stop the ball before returning it to their partners. Encourage players to relax the part of the body used for stopping the ball, as this relaxation will have a cushioning effect.

32

By stopping the ball players will improve the accuracy of passes, because it's easier to strike a stationary ball than one in motion. Level 2 incorporates movement after the pass. This movement helps to establish the concept that the passer should continue to be a player (instead of becoming a spectator) after passing. Later this movement will lead to executing wall passes.

RELATED DRILLS

33, 34

33 THREAD-THE-NEEDLE DRILL

PURPOSE

To improve passing accuracy and collection skills from a stationary passer to a stationary target with no defensive pressure.

LEVEL

Beginner, advanced beginner

EQUIPMENT

One soccer ball and two game markers for every two players

TIME

5 minutes

PROCEDURE

1. Partners with two cones between them scatter over the field (see figure).
2. Place cones initially about 3 or 4 yards apart.
3. Partners pass the ball to each other between the markers.
4. Have some fun with this drill by making it a game.
5. On the coach's signal, players begin passing.
6. After each successful pass, they take one step backward.
7. If the ball does not go between the markers, players must return to the starting point and begin again.
8. After 2 minutes, stop and see how far apart partners are.

KEY POINTS

Begin this drill with partners approximately 10 yards apart. As the skill level of the players improves, increase the distance between the players and decrease the distance between the markers. To assess player performance, count how many times the players are able to pass the ball between the markers in 20 attempts. Make sure that players collect the ball and bring it to a stop before returning the pass.

RELATED DRILLS

33, 35

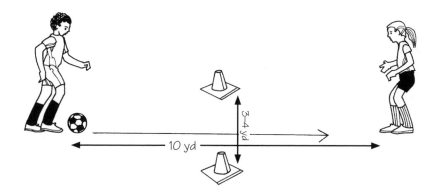

34 TUNNEL CONNECTION DRILL

PURPOSE

To improve passing accuracy and collection skills from a stationary passer to a stationary target with no defensive pressure.

LEVEL

Intermediate

EQUIPMENT

One soccer ball for every three players

TIME

5 to 7 minutes

PROCEDURE

1. Three players stand in a line, approximately 10 yards apart (see figure).
2. Player A passes the ball through player B's legs to player C.
3. Player B then switches with player A.
4. Player C passes through player A's legs to player B and then switches with player A.
5. Repeat action several times.

KEY POINTS

Encourage players to collect the ball and then wait for their partners to get to their positions before passing it. Without patience, spacing becomes a problem with this drill. If necessary, place markers at 10-yard intervals to help players with spacing.

RELATED DRILLS

32, 33

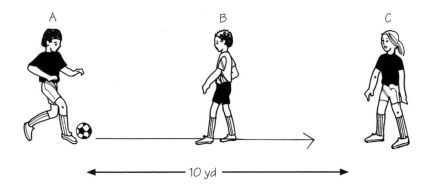

GOOD-BYE DRILL

PURPOSE

To develop passing accuracy and collection skills from a stationary passer to a stationary target, and to initiate movement after the pass with no defensive pressure.

LEVEL

Beginner

EQUIPMENT

One soccer ball and four game markers for every three players

TIME

5 to 7 minutes

PROCEDURE

Level 1

1. Position three players in a 10-yard by 10-yard grid, so that they each occupy a corner of the grid (see figure).
2. Player A passes to player B, then says good-bye and travels to the unoccupied corner of the grid.
3. Player B then passes to player C, says good-bye, and travels to the corner vacated by player A.
4. Repeat this action several times.

Level 2

1. After players feel comfortable with the spacing provided by the 10-yard grid, remove the game markers.
2. Request that all players travel in threes, repeating the movement in general space.

KEY POINTS

Encourage players to deliver crisp, flat passes that are easy to collect. Players should pass and move quickly to the open space. Reinforce this repeated action of pass and move in scrimmages and games. At level 2, encourage players to move through open spaces as they negotiate other players and to maintain 10-yard spacing.

RELATED DRILLS

None

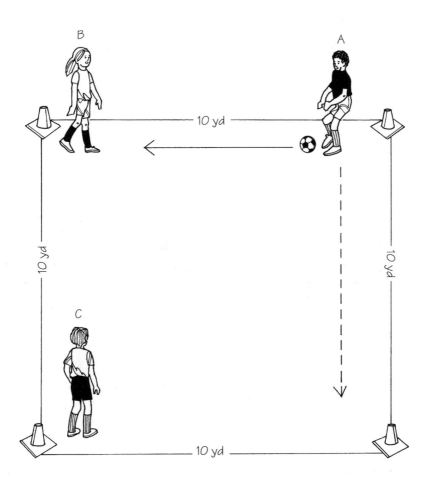

36 CIRCLE COLLECTION DRILL

PURPOSE

To develop passing accuracy and collection skills from a stationary passer to a moving target with no defensive pressure.

LEVEL

Advanced beginner, intermediate

EQUIPMENT

Six soccer balls for every nine players

TIME

10 minutes

PROCEDURE

1. Six players form a circle.
2. Each player has a ball (see figure).
3. Three other players are in constant motion inside the circle.
4. As an inside player makes eye contact with a player on the circle, the ball is passed to the inside player.
5. The inside player returns the pass to the player who passed it and moves to another space to collect another pass.
6. Players forming the circle exchange places with the inside players every 1 to 2 minutes.

KEY POINTS

Caution players moving inside the circle to pass through open spaces. Players on the inside should collect, look, and make good decisions concerning their next pass. This will help to avoid striking another moving player with the ball.

RELATED DRILLS

37, 38, 39

PURPOSE

To develop passing accuracy and collection skills from a stationary passer to a moving target with no defensive pressure.

LEVEL

Beginner

EQUIPMENT

One soccer ball and four game markers for every three players

TIME

5 to 7 minutes

PROCEDURE

Level 1

1. Each of three players stands in a corner of a 10-yard by 10-yard grid (see figure).
2. Player C, closest to the unoccupied corner and not in possession of the ball, moves to the unoccupied corner and says the word "hello."
3. Player A, the one with the ball, passes to player C.
4. Player B moves to the space vacated by player C and then receives a pass from player C.

Level 2

1. As players become comfortable with spacing, remove game markers. Several groups of players can move in one large grid, repeating level 1 action.

KEY POINTS

Coaches should encourage the players moving to a new space to give an oral reminder to the passers. In this drill they should be saying "hello." For the sake of consistency, coaches may want their players to say the word "space." The moving players should wait until the passer has controlled the ball and has made eye contact before they initiate any movement. Discuss with players how delivering a soft pass to a player who is coming toward the ball will aid the collection process.

RELATED DRILLS

36, 38, 39

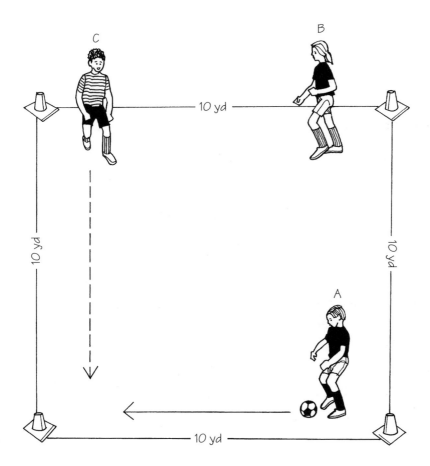

SPACEMAN DRILL

PURPOSE

To develop passing accuracy and collection skills from a stationary passer to a moving target with no defensive pressure.

LEVEL

Advanced beginner, intermediate

EQUIPMENT

One soccer ball and three game markers for every two players

TIME

5 to 7 minutes

PROCEDURE

Level 1

1. Position two players in a triangle identified by markers placed 10 yards apart.
2. Each player occupies a corner of the triangle (see figure).
3. The player without the ball runs to the unoccupied corner of the triangle and says loudly the word "space!"
4. The player with the ball passes it to the moving player.
5. The player who passed the ball moves to the unoccupied corner to receive a return pass.
6. Repeat this action several times.

Level 2

1. Remove game markers. Have partners travel through general space using a triangular pattern with 10-yard spacing.

KEY POINTS

Encourage players moving to open space to make eye contact with the passer to ensure that the passer has the ball under control to make a pass. Instruct the passer to lead the player moving to space by passing the ball slightly ahead of him, so that he doesn't have to break stride to collect the ball. Timing runs and communicating well are important to the success of this drill.

RELATED DRILLS

36, 37, 39

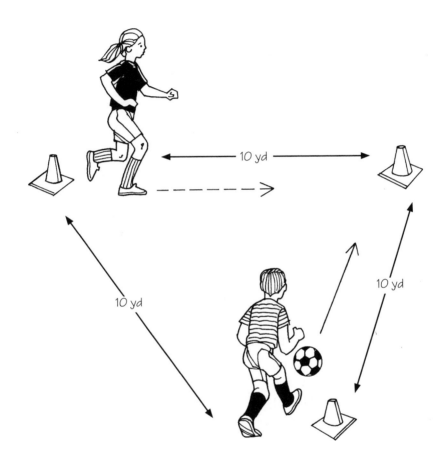

39 PENDULUM DRILL

PURPOSE

To develop passing accuracy and collection skills from a stationary passer to a moving target with no defensive pressure.

LEVEL

Advanced beginner, intermediate

EQUIPMENT

Two soccer balls and four game markers for every three players

TIME

7 to 10 minutes

PROCEDURE

1. Position three players in a 10-yard by 10-yard grid (see figure).
2. Two players, standing on one side of the grid, each have a ball.
3. A third player will be on the opposite side.
4. The player without the ball will move to the unoccupied corner.
5. As she moves, the player on that side will pass the ball.
6. The moving player will collect the ball and return it to the player who passed it to her, and then run to the corner she just left to receive a pass from the other player.
7. Continue this back-and-forth movement.
8. After 1 minute, switch roles.
9. After skills improve, play the pendulum game by counting how many passes a player can make in 1 minute.

KEY POINTS

Encourage players to make flat passes with the correct amount of force that will be easy to collect. Discuss how the speed of the player affects how far the passer must lead the pass.

RELATED DRILLS

36, 37, 38

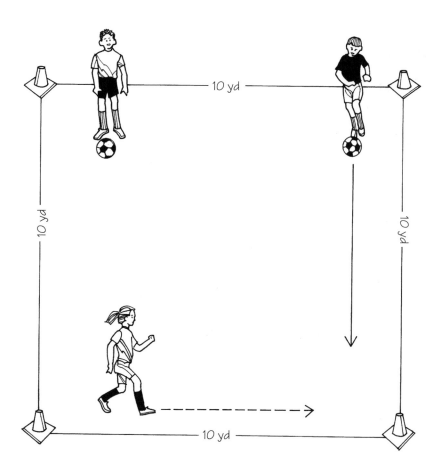

PURPOSE

To develop first-touch and passing accuracy with no defensive pressure.

LEVEL

Intermediate, advanced

EQUIPMENT

One soccer ball, two game markers

TIME

10 minutes

PROCEDURE

1. Position two game markers 5 feet apart.
2. Player A stands slightly behind and to the side of one of the markers, and player B, with the ball, stands 10 feet in front of the middle of the markers (see figure).
3. Player A moves laterally from outside the first marker to a position between the two markers. In this position, she receives a pass and first-touches the ball to the outside of the second marker. She then passes the ball to player B.
4. Players repeat the action for 1 minute and then change roles.

KEY POINTS

Emphasize the importance of using the first touch to position the ball for the next play. A good first touch often means cushioning (slowing the pace of the ball by moving the contact foot slightly backwards). A good first touch also allows the next play of the ball to occur quickly. Encourage players to use flat passes with the correct pace on the ball. Variations on this drill might include having the receiver two-touch to the outside (touch the ball twice using one foot or a combination of right and left foot), or having the receiver first-time the ball (pass the ball to a teammate on the first touch without collecting it).

RELATED DRILL

39

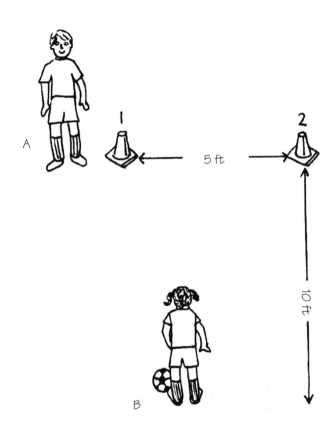

41 LINE DRILL

PURPOSE

To develop passing accuracy and collection skills from a moving player to a stationary target with no defensive pressure.

LEVEL

Intermediate

EQUIPMENT

One soccer ball and two game markers for every three players

TIME

5 minutes

PROCEDURE

1. Place two game markers 3 to 4 yards apart.
2. Position three players in a line (see figure).
3. Player B passes to player A, who collects, dribbles toward player C, and passes to player C.
4. Player C collects and dribbles toward player B, who took the place of player A.
5. Repeat this action several times.

KEY POINTS

This is a fast-paced drill that provides opportunities for lots of touches on the ball. Encourage players to make collection as easy as possible by delivering flat, soft passes.

RELATED DRILLS

36, 42, 43

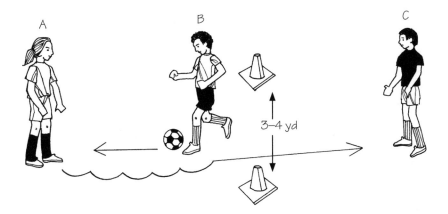

3–4 yd

42 DIAGONAL PASSING DRILL

PURPOSE

To develop passing accuracy and collection skills from a moving passer to a stationary target with no defensive pressure.

LEVEL

Intermediate

EQUIPMENT

One soccer ball and four game markers for every three players

TIME

5 minutes

PROCEDURE

Level 1

1. Position three players in a 10-yard by 10-yard grid so that each occupies a corner space (see figure).
2. Player A dribbles to the unoccupied corner and passes diagonally to player B.
3. Player B dribbles to the corner vacated by player A and passes to player C.
4. Repeat action several times.

Level 2

1. Remove the game markers.
2. Players move through general space repeating this action.

KEY POINTS

Players must use a controlled dribble to keep the ball in the grid. They must turn their nonkicking foot slightly toward the target before passing. This will allow the hips to rotate and the kicking foot to swing outside of the ball before impact. At level 2, encourage players to maintain 10-yard spacing and avoid closed spaces.

RELATED DRILLS

36, 41, 43

43 RETURN-TO-SENDER DRILL

PURPOSE

To develop passing accuracy and collection skills from a moving passer to a stationary target with no defensive pressure.

LEVEL

Intermediate, advanced

EQUIPMENT

One soccer ball for every two players, four game markers, two sets of jerseys—one jersey for each player

TIME

7 to 10 minutes

PROCEDURE

1. Scatter players in a 30-yard by 30-yard grid (see figure).
2. Half the players wear red jerseys and the other half wear green.
3. The green players, each with a ball, move freely in a grid.
4. As green players approach a stationary red player, they pass to her, collect the return pass, move through space again, and pass to another red team member.
5. Repeat for 1 minute, making as many passes as possible to different players.
6. Reverse roles.
7. Vary this drill by delivering passes at different levels.

KEY POINTS

This drill will go more smoothly for beginning players if the stationary players collect the ball with their hands and then roll it to the passer, who should be moving to a new space. As the players become more skillful, require them to collect with various body parts or to execute one-touch passes.

RELATED DRILLS

36, 41, 42

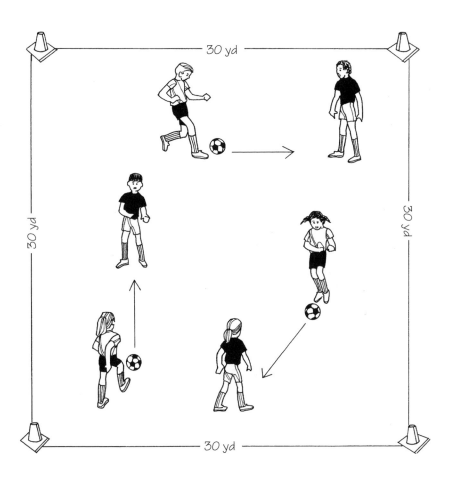

PURPOSE

To develop passing accuracy and collection skills from a moving passer to a moving target with no defensive pressure.

LEVEL

Intermediate, advanced

EQUIPMENT

One soccer ball and four game markers for every five players

TIME

5 minutes

PROCEDURE

1. Position players in a 10-yard by 10-yard grid so that four players occupy the corners of the grid (see figure).
2. Player E is outside the grid beside player A, ready to occupy that space when player A leaves.
3. Player A moves toward, and passes to, player B, who begins to move when player A reaches the halfway point between them.
4. After passing to player B, player A continues to move and occupies player B's original space.
5. Player B collects on the move and passes to player C, who begins to move when player B reaches the halfway point between them.
6. Players continue this action of collecting while moving, passing to the next player, and then occupying that player's corner of the grid.
7. As passing skills improve, challenge players by counting how many times they can pass the ball around the entire grid in 2 minutes.

KEY POINTS

Passers should make eye contact with players they are passing to and should lead them with a pass that they can easily collect. You may use more players in this drill by positioning them by the corners outside the grid. As a player completes the pass, he goes to the end of the line instead of standing by the marker.

RELATED DRILLS

45, 46

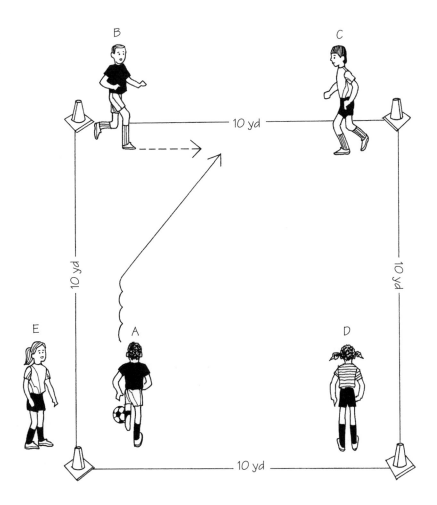

45 PASS-DRIBBLE-PASS DRILL

PURPOSE

To develop passing accuracy and collection skills from a moving passer to a moving target with no defensive pressure.

LEVEL

Intermediate, advanced

EQUIPMENT

One soccer ball and four game markers for every two players

TIME

5 minutes

PROCEDURE

Level 1

1. Position two players in a 15-yard by 15-yard grid (see figure).
2. Player A passes to player B, who dribbles into open space, turns, and then passes back to player A, who has moved to a new space behind her.
3. Repeat this action.

Level 2

1. Remove game markers.
2. Players repeat action moving in general space.

KEY POINTS

This drill requires players to pass the ball in a backward direction. Players who take space behind another player should communicate that they are in an open space by saying the word "drop." Players who pass in a backward direction should practice using the heel to pass and changing the position of the body in relation to the ball, as demonstrated in the stepover move. At level 2, encourage partners to communicate with each other so that they are not separated when all partner groups are moving in general space.

RELATED DRILLS

44, 46

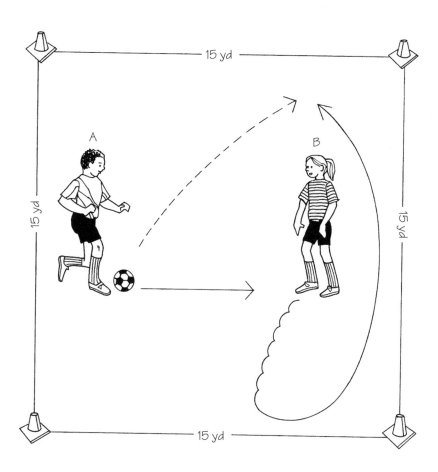

PURPOSE

To develop passing accuracy from a moving passer to a moving target with no defensive pressure.

LEVEL

Advanced

EQUIPMENT

One soccer ball for every two players and four game markers

TIME

5 to 7 minutes

PROCEDURE

1. Players scatter in pairs within a 20-yard by 20-yard grid.
2. Each set of partners has a ball (see figure).
3. On the coach's signal, the players begin to move through the grid.
4. The players with the balls pass to their partners, who must pass back on the first touch.
5. Partners continue moving, using only one-touch passing.

KEY POINTS

Players must use good visual habits to negotiate space and avoid other players. Initially partners should move with no more than 3 or 4 yards between them. As players become more proficient at one-touch passing, they can separate by greater distances.

RELATED DRILLS

44, 45

PURPOSE

To develop passing and collection skills with subtle defensive pressure.

LEVEL

Intermediate, advanced

EQUIPMENT

One soccer ball and four game markers for every three players

TIME

5 to 7 minutes

PROCEDURE

1. Position three players in a 10-yard by 10-yard grid.
2. Players are in a straight line, with players B and C looking in the direction of player A (see figure).
3. Player B can move laterally, but not forward or backward.
4. Player C moves either right or left to receive a pass from player A.
5. Player B then faces player C, and players repeat the action.
6. After several chances, change defenders.

KEY POINTS

Adding a defender (player B) subtly pressures the passer, because the defender blocks his vision. In fact, if player C does not move into open space, he is practically invisible to player A.

RELATED DRILLS

48, 49

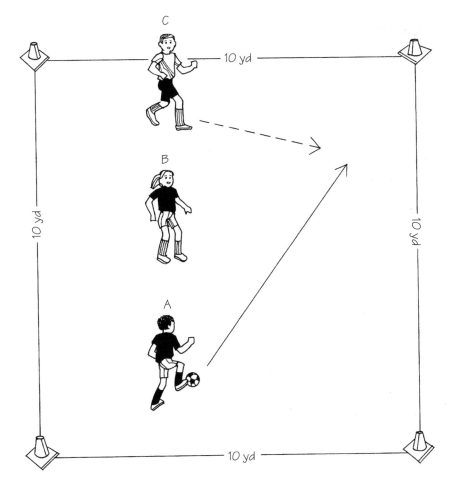

PURPOSE

To develop passing and collection skills with subtle defensive pressure.

LEVEL

Intermediate, advanced

EQUIPMENT

One soccer ball for every six players

TIME

5 minutes

PROCEDURE

1. Position five players to form five points of a star (see figure).
2. Place one defender in the middle of the star.
3. Players try to make as many consecutive passes as possible without losing control or allowing the defender to touch the ball.
4. Players may not pass the ball to the players beside them.

KEY POINTS

This is a 5 v 1 drill. The offensive players have a big advantage. Beginning players need this advantage to collect the ball, look around, and decide where and how to pass it.

RELATED DRILLS

47, 49

49 MONKEY-IN-THE-MIDDLE DRILL

PURPOSE

To develop passing and collection skills with subtle pressure, movement without the ball, and decision-making ability concerning the use of open versus closed space.

LEVEL

Advanced beginner, intermediate

EQUIPMENT

One soccer ball and four game markers for every four players

TIME

10 minutes

PROCEDURE

1. Position four game markers to make a 10-yard by 10-yard grid. Three players occupy spaces by three of the markers.

2. A fourth player is in the middle and is affectionately referred to as the "monkey" (see figure).

3. The perimeter players are playing a 3 v 1 keepaway game.

4. They may not pass the ball across the middle of the square.

5. This limitation forces them to move constantly to support positions, so that the passer always has two passing lanes from which to choose.

6. For example, if the player by cone 1 has the ball, the other two players move to spaces by cone 2 and cone 4.

7. If the player in the middle (the defender) closes the space between 1 and 2, then the pass is made to the player at cone 4.

8. The receiving players then move to cone 1 and cone 3.

9. Since a player already occupies cone 1, the player who was at cone 2 moves to cone 3 to support the passer.

10. It is impossible for the defender to close both passing lanes.

11. The defender earns his way out of the middle when he touches the ball or forces an error in passing or collecting.

KEY POINTS

Perimeter players must collect the ball, look around, and decide between passing choices. They also must communicate with each other concerning space. Variations of this drill might include limiting touches on the ball, using diagonal runs to space, or allowing dribbling to space.

RELATED DRILLS

47, 48

50

CONE DRILL

PURPOSE

To develop passing and collection skills with gamelike defensive pressure.

LEVEL

Intermediate, advanced

EQUIPMENT

One soccer ball and five game markers for every six players

TIME

8 to 10 minutes

PROCEDURE

1. Position a player on each side of a 15-yard by 15-yard grid.
2. One of these players has a ball.
3. Place a game marker in the center of the grid.
4. Two players are inside the grid (see figure).
5. One is an offensive player and the other is a defensive player.
6. The offensive player must run around the cone and sprint toward the player with the ball.
7. The player with the ball passes to the offensive player if he is in an open space.
8. If the defender closes his space, the passer instead passes to another player on the grid.
9. The offensive player repeats, going around the cone toward the new player with the ball.
10. The offensive player collects and returns the ball each time to the passer, who then passes to another player on the perimeter of the grid.

KEY POINTS

Challenge players to count how many times the offensive player receives a pass in 1 minute. Passers must give the offensive players soft passes to collect. Defensive players work hard to close the space between the offensive player and the passer. Increase the difficulty of collection by serving balls at various speeds and levels to challenge more advanced players.

RELATED DRILLS

51, 52

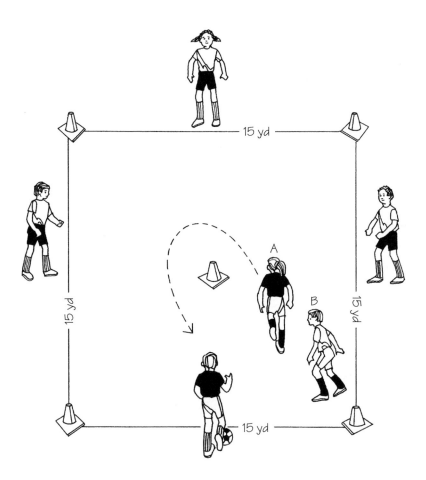

51 CHECK OUT–CHECK IN DRILL

PURPOSE

To develop passing and collection skills under gamelike defensive pressure.

LEVEL

Intermediate, advanced

EQUIPMENT

One soccer ball and four game markers for every six players

TIME

8 to 10 minutes

PROCEDURE

1. Position a player on each side of a 15-yard by 15-yard grid.
2. One player has the ball.
3. Two players (A and B) are inside the grid (see figure).
4. Player A runs away (checks out) from the ball, changes direction, and then sprints toward the ball (checks in) to receive a pass.
5. If the defender (player B) closes the space, the passer plays the ball to another player on the grid.
6. If the offensive player collects the pass, he should shield the ball for 5 to 10 seconds before returning a pass.
7. Challenge players to count how many consecutive passes the offensive player receives in 1 minute without the defensive player touching the ball.

KEY POINTS

Offensive players should move away from the ball at a moderate rate of speed. After changing directions, they should accelerate toward the ball. Changing speeds makes denying space more difficult for the defender.

RELATED DRILLS

50, 52

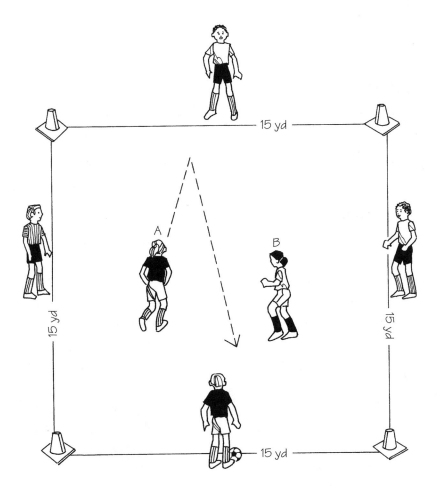

52   BEAT-THE-CLOCK DRILL

PURPOSE

To develop passing and collecting skills under gamelike defensive pressure.

LEVEL

Advanced

EQUIPMENT

One soccer ball for every two players, four game markers, and two sets of different colored jerseys (one jersey for each player)

TIME

8 to 10 minutes

PROCEDURE

1. Divide the group into two equal teams wearing jerseys of two different colors.
2. Position team A players, each with a ball, inside a 30-yard by 30-yard grid.
3. Members of team B are outside the grid.
4. On the coach's signal, players on team B enter the grid, try to gain possession of a ball, and kick it out of the grid (see figure).
5. After a team A player's ball is kicked out of the grid, he goes to a support position so that a teammate can pass him a ball.
6. The coach times how long it takes the defensive team to get all the balls out of the grid.
7. The teams then switch roles.

KEY POINTS

Team A players should move to open space to maintain possession of the ball. Should they lose possession, they should move to a support position where they will try to collect, look around, and make a good decision about where to play the ball next.

RELATED DRILLS

50, 51

53   1 V 1 DRILL

PURPOSE

To develop decision-making abilities concerning passing choices under gamelike defensive pressure.

LEVEL

Intermediate, advanced

EQUIPMENT

One soccer ball, one jersey for defender, two jerseys (different color from defender jersey) for neutral players, and four game markers for every four players

TIME

8 to 10 minutes

PROCEDURE

Level 1

1. Position four players in a 15-yard by 15-yard grid—one offensive, one defensive, and two neutral players (see figure).
2. The offensive player passes to one of the neutral players and then moves to open space to receive a return pass.
3. Players try to connect as many consecutive passes as possible.
4. If the defender gains possession, he becomes the offensive player.
5. After 1 minute of possession, switch roles.

Level 2

1. Use only one neutral player.
2. Apply a two-touch limit.

KEY POINTS

Players must quickly change speed and direction to create space for passes. Variations of this drill include adding players to make 2 v 2 or 3 v 3. Add goals to encourage finishing skills. Neutral players may not be defended against.

RELATED DRILLS

None

54   KEEPAWAY DRILL

PURPOSE

To develop the techniques and tactics used by the second attacker.

LEVEL

Intermediate, advanced

EQUIPMENT

One ball, four game markers, and one red jersey

TIME

10 minutes

PROCEDURE

1. Position four game markers to make a 20-yard by 20-yard grid.
2. Three players are positioned inside the grid—two offensive players and one defensive player in the red jersey (see figure).
3. On the coach's signal, the two offensive players try to maintain possession of the ball while the player with the red jersey defends.
4. After 1 minute, or if the defender is successful in either gaining possession or causing the ball to be played outside of the grid, switch roles.

KEY POINTS

Initially players who assume the role of the second attacker tend to run away from the ball, attempting to move as far away from the defender as possible. Teach players instead to assume a position of close support (the role of the second attacker) that will enable them to work with the first attacker to confuse the defender. Encourage the use of the wall pass, the takeover, and the overlap pass. For a wall pass, the second attacker receives a short pass, immediately executes another short pass behind the defender and close to the first attacker, collects the ball, and continues to run. When executing a takeover, the second attacker runs behind and close to the first attacker, collects the ball, and continues to run. In the overlap pass, the second attacker runs behind the first attacker and continues a curved run forward, at an angle wide enough for her to receive a pass. Variations of this drill include adding a server outside of the grid to initiate action by serving the ball on the ground or in the air, or by throwing the ball in. You can also change the drill by restricting the number of touches on the ball by the offensive players (for example, two touches). Or you can add more structure, requiring the two offensive players to move the ball from one end line to the other under a time constraint (for example, 20 seconds).

RELATED DRILLS
55, 56

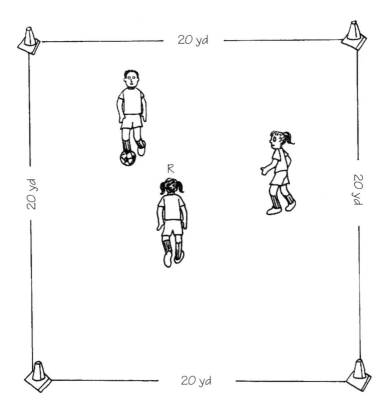

55   2 V 2 KEEPAWAY DRILL

PURPOSE

To develop the techniques and tactics used by the second attacker.

LEVEL

Intermediate, advanced

EQUIPMENT

One ball, four game markers, four jerseys (two blue, two red)

TIME

10 minutes

PROCEDURE

1. Position four game markers to make a 20-yard by 20-yard grid.
2. Four players are in the grid, two red and two blue (see figure).
3. On the coach's signal, the two offensive players try to keep the ball away from the two defensive players.
4. After 1 minute, or if the defensive players gain possession of the ball or cause it to be played outside of the grid, switch roles.

KEY POINTS

Encourage offensive players to confuse the defenders with creative moves by the second attacker, who can provide opportunities for ball passes, takeovers, and overlaps. Vary the drill by requiring the team in possession of the ball to move from one end of the grid to the other within a time restriction (such as 30 seconds). This drill also develops the roles of the first defender (who defends against the player with the ball, denying penetration) and the second defender (who defends against the offensive teammate closest to the player with the ball, providing cover for the first defender). Select this drill as either an offensive or defensive tool for instruction, but do not confuse players by commenting on both aspects of play at the same time.

RELATED DRILLS

54, 56

56 TWO-TEAMMATE PASSING GAME

PURPOSE

To develop the techniques and tactics used by the second attacker.

LEVEL

Intermediate, advanced

EQUIPMENT

One ball, four game markers, twelve jerseys (six red, six blue)

TIME

20 minutes

PROCEDURE

1. Position four game markers to make a 20-yard by 30-yard grid.
2. Inside the grid, position two red and two blue players. One team starts with the ball.
3. Position one red and one blue player on each 20-yard end and each 30-yard side of the grid (see figure).
4. On the coach's whistle, the team in possession of the ball tries to pass the ball to a teammate on either end of the grid.
5. The end player will pass the ball back to one of her teammates inside the grid.
6. Teammates inside the grid will then pass the ball to the teammate on the opposite end.
7. Each successful pass to one end player and then the other, maintaining possession of the ball, results in 1 point for that team.
8. After 3 minutes rotate inside players to the side, side players to the end, and end players to the inside of the grid.
9. Repeat the action.

KEY POINTS

This is a passing drill, so limit players to three touches on the ball. Encourage the inside players to make quick give-and-go passes to their teammates on the sides. Also, remind the inside players that the second attacker works with the first attacker (the one with the ball) to penetrate the defense. Review positioning and movements of the second attacker. She should stay close enough to work with the first attacker using short passes, but far away enough that one defender cannot successfully defend against both players. Remind them that this sort of teamwork allows creative plays such as wall passes, takeovers, and overlaps. Sideline and endline players do not defend each other.

RELATED DRILLS

54, 55

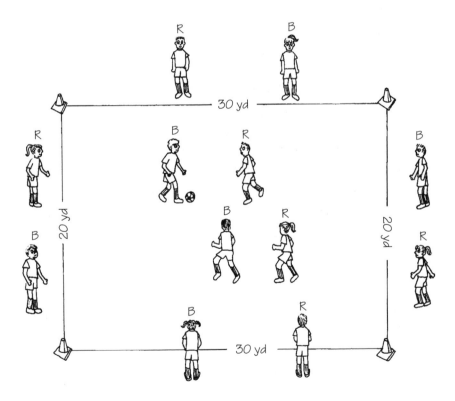

57   3 V 2 LINE GAME

PURPOSE

To develop the techniques and tactics used by the third attacker.

LEVEL

Intermediate, advanced

EQUIPMENT

One ball, four game markers, six jerseys (three red, three blue)

TIME

10 minutes

PROCEDURE

1. Position four game markers to make a 20-yard by 40-yard grid.
2. Position three offensive players (red) and two defensive players (blue) inside the grid. A third blue player is positioned outside of the grid by side 2 (see figure).
3. On the coach's signal, the three red players try to keep the ball in their possession while moving the ball from side 1 to side 2 of the grid. If successful, they earn 1 point.
4. If the red team is successful, or if they lose possession of the ball, one of them must go outside of the grid by side 1. The third blue player enters from side 2. The blue team now tries to move the ball from side 2 to side 1.
5. Repeat the action.

KEY POINTS

This drill enables players to develop the role of the third attacker, which is to create space to receive the ball behind the defenders. Encourage the player who is not being defended against to make wide, bending runs to attract the defenders' attention and cause confusion. Restrict touches on the ball by the offensive team at first, which will necessitate less dribbling and more passing.

RELATED DRILLS

None

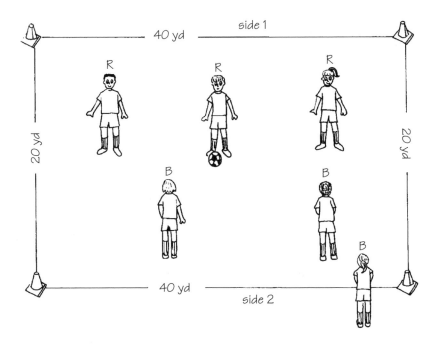

58 THREE-TEAM PASSING DRILL

PURPOSE

To develop passing accuracy with no defensive pressure.

LEVEL

Intermediate, advanced

EQUIPMENT

Three soccer balls, four game markers, twelve jerseys (four red, four blue, four green)

TIME

10 minutes

PROCEDURE

1. Position four game markers to make a 30-yard by 30-yard grid.
2. Twelve players divided into three teams (red, blue, and green) scatter in the grid, four players per team (see figure). One player from each team has a ball.
3. On the coach's signal, players move throughout the grid passing to teammates.

KEY POINTS

Encourage players to move to open spaces to support the player with the ball, and to communicate between teammates. Good visual scanning will enable players to find the open spaces. Variations of this drill might include numbering players on each team to pass consecutively (number 1 passes to number 2, and so forth), requiring players to pass between two like opponents (two red players, two blue players), restricting the number of touches (two touches, one touch), or using two balls for each team. Encourage players to use the entire width and depth of the grid as they move. Note that teams do not play defense during this drill.

RELATED DRILLS

59, 60

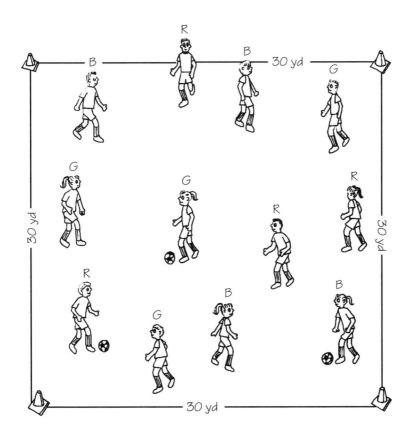

TWO-TEAM KEEPAWAY DRILL

PURPOSE

To develop passing accuracy with gamelike defensive pressure.

LEVEL

Intermediate, advanced

EQUIPMENT

One ball, six game markers, eight jerseys (four blue, four red)

TIME

10 minutes

PROCEDURE

1. Position six game markers to make two 20-yard by 20-yard grids side by side.
2. Four blue players scatter in grid 1. One player has a ball (see figure).
3. The four red players scatter in grid 2.
4. On the coach's signal, the blue team tries to connect as many passes as possible. Every time they connect five passes in a row, they earn 1 point.
5. On the coach's signal to begin play, the red team sends two players (defenders) into grid 1.
6. If the red players touch the ball or cause it to be played outside of the grid, the red team gains possession of the ball.
7. The red defender closest to the ball is then allowed one free pass to a teammate in grid 2. Blue players must freeze until the ball is played to grid 2, at which time they may send two defenders to try to prevent the red team from connecting passes.
8. Action is repeated.

KEY POINTS

This is a tactical (decision-making) exercise using passing techniques. Encourage players to use vision, communication, and movement to keep the ball away from their opponents. Emphasize the importance of spacing players across the depth and width of the grid. Limit dribbling initially to three touches on the ball. As players develop, impose a no-dribble rule.

RELATED DRILLS

58, 60

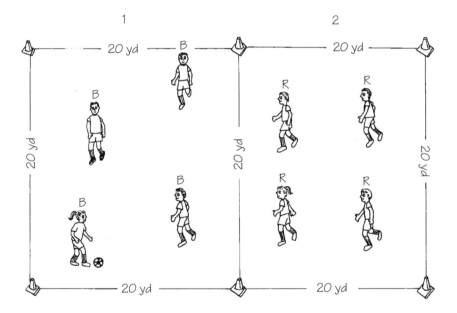

60 THREE-TEAM KEEPAWAY DRILL

PURPOSE

To develop passing accuracy under subtle defensive pressure.

LEVEL

Advanced

EQUIPMENT

One soccer ball, four game markers, nine jerseys (three red, three yellow, three blue)

TIME

10 minutes

PROCEDURE

1. Position four game markers to make a 30-yard by 30-yard square.
2. Divide nine players into three teams of three players. Each team wears different colored jerseys (see figure).
3. The red and blue teams begin passing to each other while keeping the ball away from the yellow team. The yellow team plays defense, trying to recover possession of the ball.
4. If the yellow team gains possession or the ball is played outside of the grid, the team who made the mistake must now play defense.
5. If the red team is on defense, the yellow team combines with the blue to keep the ball away from the red.
6. The action is repeated, with two teams passing the ball while keeping it away from the third team.

KEY POINTS

This activity offers a numbers advantage (more players) for the two teams in possession of the ball. This advantage increases the likelihood of successfully connecting passes between players. To help players become more successful in keeping the ball away from one opponent, encourage them to use good visual scanning techniques.

This will help them see players in open spaces to whom they may pass. Emphasize to players without the ball that movement to open spaces creates passing opportunities. Encourage the second attacker (teammate closest to the player with the ball) to provide close support and the third attackers (all teammates who are not the first and second attackers) to provide width, depth, and mobility.

RELATED DRILLS

58, 59

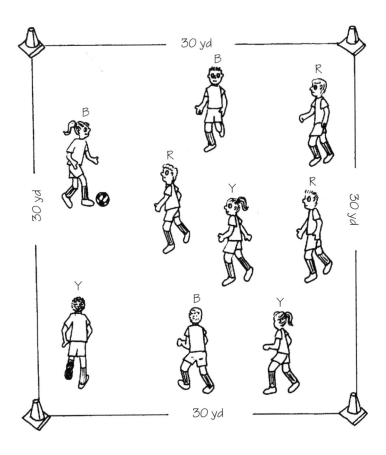

4

Heading Drills

Heading is a method of controlling the ball to pass or shoot. Like any other pass or shot, proper execution of this skill involves many concepts.

The intended direction or pathway of the ball determines what part of the ball the player should apply force to, what part of the head should apply the force, and how much force other body parts should generate. For example, if a player wants to head the ball toward the ground, she strikes the ball with a downward motion of her forehead. If she wants the ball to go upward, she can strike the bottom portion of the ball with the forehead. She can also use the top of the head to play the ball in a backward direction. If a player wants the ball to travel to the right, she has a choice of either using the right side of her head to strike it or maneuvering her body before the ball arrives and using her forehead to strike it. The opposite would apply for a ball that the player wants to play to the left.

The amount of force that a player should use on the ball is determined by how far the ball must travel after contact. A player generates force by bending at the waist and snapping the head and shoulders in a forward action.

The position of the ball in relation to the player and the position of the player on the field are other factors that help determine proper heading techniques. Players in the defensive third of the field generally head the ball high and wide, away from their goal. Players in the midfield should play the ball more precisely, as they are often trying to head it to attacking players. Players in the offensive third of the field use heading skills mainly for scoring opportunities. Placement, not power, is essential for these players.

Most beginning players must overcome the fear of being struck in the face by the ball. When teaching heading skills, address this concern by using a sponge-type ball. In some cases it may be necessary to use a slightly larger and lighter ball (similar to a beach ball) to reduce fear. The teaching progression for heading is as follows:

1. No defensive pressure, tossing softly to self from knees
2. Standing tossing to self
3. Standing with partner tossing

4. Heading with subtle defensive pressure
5. Heading with gamelike defensive pressure

Begin the heading progression by positioning players on their knees to ensure proper balance of the lower body. Players can then concentrate on the action of the upper body. As the players feel more comfortable striking the ball with their heads, they can move to a standing position. At this stage players begin to learn about the contributions the lower body makes to heading.

For the next step in the progression, partners toss the ball to each other while stationary and then while in motion. Emphasize positioning the body to get under the ball at this level. As players gain more confidence, have them jump and head the ball using a one-foot takeoff. Challenge them by offering heading drills with subtle and gamelike defensive pressure. Refining heading skills is another step toward adding more structure to the game and developing intentional play.

61   TOSS-TO-SELF HEADING DRILL

PURPOSE

To develop the skill of striking the ball with the part of the forehead known as the hairline, with no defensive pressure.

LEVEL

Beginner, advanced beginner

EQUIPMENT

One foam ball or beach ball for every player

TIME

5 to 7 minutes

PROCEDURE

Level 1

1. Position players in a scattered formation.
2. Players should be on their knees, each with a ball. Players toss the ball slightly above their heads (see figure), strike it gently with their heads, and then catch the ball before it hits the ground.
3. Repeat several times.

Level 2

1. After players have demonstrated correct heading techniques, have them repeat this action from a standing position.

KEY POINTS

Show players the location of the hairline. Emphasize moving the head to strike the ball instead of merely positioning the head so the ball will hit it. Insist that players strike the ball with their eyes open and mouths closed. This practice will prevent them from biting their tongues later when using a harder ball. At level 2, encourage players to establish a good base of support by flexing their knees slightly and positioning their feet a little more than shoulder-width apart.

RELATED DRILLS

62, 63

62   PARTNER HEADING DRILL

PURPOSE

To develop proper heading technique with no defensive pressure.

LEVEL

Beginner, advanced beginner

EQUIPMENT

One foam, sponge, or beach ball for every two players, four game markers

TIME

5 minutes

PROCEDURE

Level 1

1. Position partners in a 30-yard by 30-yard grid (see figure).
2. Each pair of players has a ball.
3. The player with the ball tosses to himself and heads the ball to his partner, who will catch, toss, and head it back.

Level 2

1. Instead of tossing to himself, the player tosses to his partner, who returns the ball by heading.
2. Players should be about 5 yards apart to begin this phase of the drill.
3. Gradually increase distance as both tossing and heading skills improve.

Level 3

1. The partner tosses to the player in motion, who returns the ball by heading.
2. The player in motion should vary directions forward, backward, left, and right.

KEY POINTS

Partners should select a type of ball with which they feel comfortable. Teach them to generate more force by bending backward at the waist and then thrusting forward to contact the ball. Players should flex knees and extend arms to improve balance.

RELATED DRILLS

61, 63

63 SHORT AND LONG HEADING DRILL

PURPOSE

To develop force relationships when heading with no defensive pressure.

LEVEL

Intermediate, advanced

EQUIPMENT

Two soccer balls and four game markers for every three players

TIME

5 to 7 minutes

PROCEDURE

Level 1

1. Position three players in a 10-yard by 10-yard grid.
2. Players B and C each have a ball (see figure).
3. Player B takes a position 5 yards from player A, and player C takes a position 10 yards from player A. Player B tosses to player A, who returns the ball by heading. Then player C tosses his ball to player A, and player A repeats the heading action.

Level 2

1. After the first toss, only heading skills may be used to pass the ball.
2. Player B tosses to player A.
3. Player A heads to player C.
4. Player C heads to player A, who returns the ball by heading to player B.
5. Repeat this action.

KEY POINTS

Players need to learn to generate different amounts of force because of the various distances the ball must travel. Emphasize that the speed with which the head strikes the ball is the major factor in generating this force. Players can increase head speed by bending at the waist and thrusting the upper body forward. At level 2, use only one ball. Encourage players to move their feet to get into good position for striking the ball.

RELATED DRILLS

61, 62

64 STAR HEADING DRILL

PURPOSE

To improve heading skills used to change ball direction, with no defensive pressure at level 1 and with subtle defensive pressure at level 2.

LEVEL

Intermediate, advanced

EQUIPMENT

One soccer ball and one game marker for every five players

TIME

5 to 7 minutes

PROCEDURE

Level 1

1. Position players in a star formation, approximately 7 to 10 yards apart.
2. Place a game marker in the middle of the star (see figure).
3. The player with the ball calls another player's name, who must run around the marker and head the tossed ball to another player.
4. Continue this action.

Level 2

1. Repeat level 1, procedures 1 through 4.
2. Add a player in the middle of the star to provide subtle defensive pressure.

KEY POINTS

Encourage players to elevate before striking the ball. Insist that players head the ball in forward, backward, left, and right directions. The defensive player should be passive and should not challenge in the air for the ball.

RELATED DRILL

65

65 THREE-CORNER HEADING DRILL

PURPOSE

To improve heading skills used to change ball direction, with no defensive pressure at level 1 and subtle defensive pressure at level 2.

LEVEL

Intermediate, advanced

EQUIPMENT

One soccer ball and four game markers for every three players

TIME

5 to 7 minutes

PROCEDURE

Level 1

1. Position three players on the corners of a 10-yard by 10-yard grid (see figure).
2. Player A tosses the ball to player B.
3. Player B heads the ball to player C, who has moved to the open corner of the grid.
4. After player A tosses, she moves to the corner originally occupied by player C.
5. Player C tosses to player A, who heads the ball to moving player B.
6. Repeat several times.

Level 2

1. Repeat level 1, procedures 1 through 5.
2. Add defenders on the outside of the grid.

KEY POINTS

Emphasize that players should lead their teammates by heading the ball to a location slightly in front of them, the same as they do when passing with the feet. Adding defending players on the outside of the grid encourages more precision with tosses and heading passes. Defenders are not allowed inside the grid and should subtly challenge in the air for head balls.

RELATED DRILL

58

66 JACK-IN-THE-BOX DRILL

PURPOSE

To improve heading skills under subtle defensive pressure.

LEVEL

Advanced

EQUIPMENT

One soccer ball and two game markers for every three players

TIME

5 minutes

PROCEDURE

1. Position three players in a line.
2. Players A and C are approximately 10 yards apart, while player B occupies a position halfway between them (see figure).
3. Player A tosses over player B to player C, who returns the ball by heading.
4. Repeat several times and change roles.

KEY POINTS

Player B provides subtle defensive pressure by obstructing the vision of player C. To add more defensive pressure, have player B jump as the ball is tossed. As the players' skills improve, reduce the distance between players B and C, and increase the distance between players A and C. Game markers help provide proper spacing so players do not drift too far apart.

RELATED DRILLS

64, 65

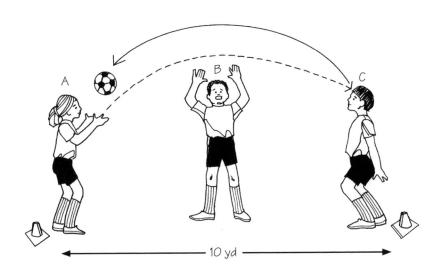

SHOW-FOR-ME DRILL

PURPOSE

To develop heading skills under gamelike defensive pressure.

LEVEL

Advanced

EQUIPMENT

One soccer ball and four game markers for every three players

TIME

5 to 7 minutes

PROCEDURE

1. Position three players in a 10-yard by 10-yard grid (see figure).
2. Player B runs away from the ball, then quickly changes speed and direction, coming back toward the ball.
3. Player A tosses the ball for player B to return by heading.
4. Player C challenges player B for the tossed ball.

KEY POINTS

Player C must not take a ball-side position on the initial run by player B. Encourage player C to move to a ball-side position and make the first touch only after player B changes direction and moves toward the ball.

RELATED DRILLS

None

5

Shooting Drills

Young players have the most fun when they are scoring goals. Practice sessions should include lots of opportunities for them to practice scoring. You can make these opportunities available during full-field scrimmages, small-sided games, and shooting drills. During full-field and small-sided games, vary procedures to encourage more goal scoring. Include games with no goalkeepers, or restrict the movement of goalkeepers with restraining lines. Adding more goals (or enlarging the ones being used) is another possibility for increasing goal production.

Goal production also increases when players improve their shooting technique (how) and tactical knowledge (when and where). As with passing skills, introduce shooting techniques as early as the beginner stage but emphasize them more strongly in the later stages of development. One of the ways to improve shooting skills is through drill work. Shooting drills develop the shooting skills players need to score goals successfully. Develop your players' shooting skills progressively. The drills in this chapter are designed to improve shooting skills using the following progression:

1. Stationary ball shot by a stationary player
2. Stationary ball shot by a moving player
3. Moving ball shot by a stationary player
4. Moving ball shot by a moving player
5. Shooting opportunities with subtle, then gamelike, defensive pressure.

Players need to learn how to strike the ball properly when shooting. Players can often take shots from close range with the inside of the foot, much like they shoot a pass. Using the inside of the foot enhances shooting accuracy. When more power is necessary, teach players to strike the ball using the instep of the foot, with toes pointed downward and ankle locked. Placement of the nonkicking foot affects the elevation of the shot. Players should learn to place the nonkicking foot slightly ahead of the ball to keep the shot low. To focus your players' attention on striking the ball, eliminate distractions such as moving balls, moving shooters, or defenders.

Begin the drill progression with a stationary ball and a stationary shooter.

As shooting techniques improve, increase the challenge by putting the shooter in motion before she strikes the ball. Such motion will distract from the precision of striking efforts initially, because the player's vision must serve a dual purpose. It must both help her negotiate space on her way to the ball, and help her place her foot at the correct location on the ball.

As players gain confidence, increase the challenge by placing both shooter and ball in motion, creating a more gamelike situation. Make this transition easier for players by serving balls that are not bouncing, at a moderate speed. When their shooting competence improves, serve balls at various speeds and levels.

The final step in the progression of drills requires developing tactical knowledge by adding defensive pressure. Begin with subtle pressure and graduate to more gamelike pressure. Keep these drills fast paced, and avoid having players stand in line, by using many balls and all available goals. If necessary, create temporary goals. You may want to incorporate shooting drills as part of a circuit in which some team members practice shooting while others practice fast footwork, passing, and so forth.

68 PARTNER STATIONARY SHOOTING DRILL

PURPOSE

To develop proper kicking techniques for shooting a stationary ball from a stationary position with no defensive pressure.

LEVEL

Beginner, advanced beginner

EQUIPMENT

One soccer ball for every two players

TIME

7 to 10 minutes

PROCEDURE

1. Players scatter and partners stand 10 to 15 yards apart.
2. The partner without the ball assumes a goalkeeper's stance, with hands in a ready position (see figure).
3. The other partner approaches the stationary ball and shoots, trying to hit his partner.

KEY POINTS

Beginning players are sometimes inaccurate while shooting. It may be necessary to increase the number of goalkeepers a player is shooting toward, so that they all spend less time chasing errant balls. For example, space three goalkeepers in ready positions about 10 feet apart, and have the shooter aim for the middle one. Reinforce the importance of accuracy over power during this drill. Encourage players to watch their foot strike the ball, and remind them to kick with the instep of the foot as opposed to the toes.

RELATED DRILLS

69, 70

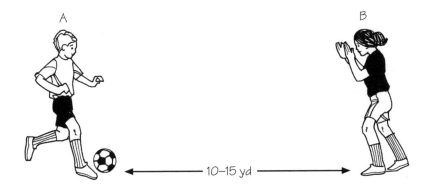

← 10–15 yd →

69 THREE-PLAYER SHOOTING DRILL

PURPOSE

To develop proper kicking technique for shooting a stationary ball from a stationary position, with no defensive pressure.

LEVEL

Advanced beginner, intermediate

EQUIPMENT

One soccer ball for every three players

TIME

7 to 10 minutes

PROCEDURE

1. Three players stand in a line approximately 10 yards apart (see figure).
2. Player A shoots the ball at player B, who is in a goalkeeper's stance.
3. Player B collects the ball and rolls it to player C.
4. Player C stops the ball and then shoots at player B.
5. After several shots, rotate players.

KEY POINTS

Emphasize striking a stationary ball with the instep of the foot. Promote the philosophy of shooting accuracy over shooting power. As the players become more competent with shooting skills, increase the distance between players.

RELATED DRILLS

68, 70

A

B

C

OPEN-CORNER DRILL

PURPOSE

To develop shooting accuracy from a stationary position with a stationary ball and no defensive pressure.

LEVEL

Beginner, advanced beginner

EQUIPMENT

One soccer ball per player, four goals

TIME

10 to 12 minutes

PROCEDURE

Level 1

1. Place several balls in a row approximately 12 to 15 yards from the goal (see figure).
2. Players shoot the balls into the unoccupied goal.

Level 2

1. Repeat level 1, procedures 1 and 2.
2. Place a goalkeeper slightly to one side of the goal.
3. Challenge the players to shoot to the unoccupied corner.

KEY POINTS

Once players have developed a proper kicking technique, they should develop an understanding of placement. During level 1 of this drill, encourage players to shoot for the corners. When you add a goalkeeper at level 2, restrict the keeper's movement by using game markers to establish how far he may move on the goal line. Players can perform this drill as part of small-group work using portable or temporary goals, or as part of station work when they are arriving at practice. Using the drill in large-group work will result in too much standing.

RELATED DRILLS

68, 69

12–15 yd

RUN-AND-SHOOT DRILL

PURPOSE

To develop proper kicking technique when the shooter is in motion, the ball is stationary, and there is no defensive pressure.

LEVEL

Advanced beginner, intermediate

EQUIPMENT

Four soccer balls, one goal, and four game markers for every four players

TIME

10 to 12 minutes

PROCEDURE

Level 1

1. Place the four balls in a row in a 15-yard by 15-yard grid.
2. The shooter runs around one of the markers and shoots the ball into the goal.
3. Repeat several times, with the shooter running around a different marker each time.

Level 2

1. Repeat level 1, procedures 1 and 2.
2. Place a goalkeeper outside each goal post (see figure).
3. As the shooter makes the turn around the marker, signal one of the goalkeepers to step into one corner of the goal.
4. The shooter must shoot to the unoccupied corner.

KEY POINTS

Requiring the shooter to run around different markers varies the angle of the kick. During level 2 action, goalkeepers must step just inside the goal on their side. This means shooters must look up to determine where to place the ball. During level 1, one player shoots, two players retrieve balls, and one player resets the balls for the next shooter. During level 2, one player shoots, two act as goalkeepers, and one retrieves balls. Coaches may want to use this drill as a station for circuit training. If you use this drill as a large-group activity, use both regular and temporary goals. Emphasize shooting low at the temporary goals and high at the regular goals.

RELATED DRILLS

None

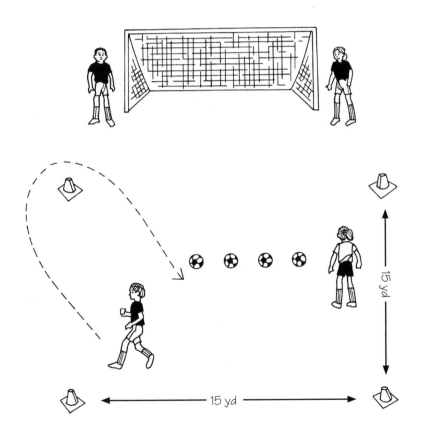

72 REVERSE SERVING SHOOTING DRILL

PURPOSE

To develop proper kicking technique for shooting a moving ball when the player is stationary and there is no defensive pressure.

LEVEL

Advanced beginner, intermediate, advanced

EQUIPMENT

Six soccer balls and two goals for every five players

TIME

12 to 15 minutes

PROCEDURE

1. Position two goals approximately 30 yards apart.
2. Place two players, D and B, on the sides with several balls.
3. Player C is the shooter (see figure).
4. When player B serves the ball, player C shoots at goalkeeper A.
5. When player D serves the ball, player C reverses and shoots at goalkeeper E.
6. After six shots everyone rotates.

KEY POINTS

This drill is more gamelike and highlights the role of target players. Putting the ball in motion reduces the shooter's time for making decisions. Point out that shooters visually track the path of their foot as it strikes the ball and must also adjust for the speed, direction, and level of the ball. To make this process less complicated for less skilled players, serve balls at a moderate speed and a flat level. As their skills improve, they may practice shooting balls served at various speeds and levels.

RELATED DRILL

73

30 yd

PASS-AND-SHOOT DRILL

PURPOSE

To develop proper kicking technique for shooting a moving ball when the player is stationary and there is no defensive pressure.

LEVEL

Advanced beginner, intermediate, advanced

EQUIPMENT

One or more soccer balls and two goals for every four players

TIME

12 to 15 minutes

PROCEDURE

1. Place two goals 30 yards apart.
2. Position players as shown (see figure).
3. Player B serves to player C, who shoots at goalkeeper D.
4. Goalkeeper D passes to player C. Player C passes to player B, who shoots at goalkeeper A.
5. Repeat several times and then change roles.

KEY POINTS

Keep several balls in the goals for goalkeepers to pass, so that the drill stays fast paced. Encourage one-touch shooting to the corners of the goals.

RELATED DRILL

72

30 yd

74 ALTERNATING SHOOTING DRILL

PURPOSE

To develop proper kicking technique for shooting a moving ball when the player is moving and there is no defensive pressure.

LEVEL

Intermediate, advanced

EQUIPMENT

Four soccer balls and one set of goals for every four players

TIME

8 to 10 minutes

PROCEDURE

1. Place two goals 30 yards apart.
2. Position two players in the center of the field (see figure).
3. Player B serves balls alternately right and left.
4. Player A must go after the ball and shoot at the goal toward which the ball is traveling.
5. Player A then returns to shoot in the opposite direction.

KEY POINTS

Moving players who are shooting moving balls must gather a lot of information in a short time. They must compute the direction, speed, and level of the ball; their speed; their angle to the ball; their level relative to the ball; the distance from goal; and the position of the goalkeeper. These complex requirements put the moving ball-moving player phase last in the shooting progression.

RELATED DRILL

75

75 SPIN-TURN SHOOTING DRILL

PURPOSE

To develop the ability to create space for shooting a moving ball when the player is moving and there is no defensive pressure.

LEVEL

Intermediate, advanced

EQUIPMENT

One soccer ball and one goal for every two players

TIME

8 to 10 minutes

PROCEDURE

1. Position players in the offensive third of the field.
2. Player A, in the penalty box, makes a horizontal run and then checks back for the ball (see figure).
3. Player B passes to player A, who returns the ball to player B with a one-touch pass.
4. After returning the pass, player A spins to the outside to create space for player B to return the pass for a shot.

KEY POINTS

Players should pivot on the inside foot (the foot closest to the goal) when spinning to the outside. Players should alternate between spinning wide, to create enough space for a pass, and spinning close to the defender to get behind him.

RELATED DRILLS

None

76 3 V 1 SHOOTING DRILL

PURPOSE

To develop proper kicking techniques for shooting a moving ball when the player is moving and there is subtle defensive pressure.

LEVEL

Intermediate, advanced

EQUIPMENT

One soccer ball and one goal for every four players, one jersey for every goalkeeper

TIME

10 to 12 minutes

PROCEDURE

Level 1

1. Position players approximately 30 yards from the goal (see figure).
2. Offensive players A, B, and C connect a series of passes until one of them takes a shot for the goal.
3. One defender provides subtle pressure.

Level 2

1. Repeat level 1, procedures 1 and 2.
2. Add a goalkeeper to provide more defensive pressure.

KEY POINTS

Each offensive player must touch the ball before one of them takes a shot. Encourage creative movements such as switching and overlapping runs. To encourage goal scoring, give the offensive players a numbers advantage such as this drill provides.

RELATED DRILLS

None

77 CAT-AND-MOUSE SHOOTING DRILL

PURPOSE

To develop abilities to create space for shooting with subtle defensive pressure.

LEVEL

Intermediate, advanced

EQUIPMENT

One soccer ball and one goal for every two players

TIME

8 to 10 minutes

PROCEDURE

1. Position players as shown in the figure.
2. Player A passes to player B.
3. Player A then makes a bending run to offer passive defense against player B's penetrating moves.
4. Player B will collect the ball and complete one or more individual moves to create space for a shot.

KEY POINTS

Player A must wait for player B to collect the ball before making his bending run. Emphasize subtle pressure by the defender since this is an offensive drill. Encourage a variety of individual moves by offensive players. To allow more scoring, do not use a goalkeeper initially. Use as many goals as possible.

RELATED DRILL

78

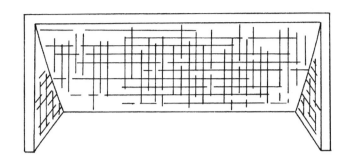

A

B

78   COME-AND-GET-ME SHOOTING DRILL

PURPOSE

To develop abilities to create space for shooting with subtle defensive pressure.

LEVEL

Intermediate, advanced

EQUIPMENT

One soccer ball and one goal for every three players

TIME

8 to 10 minutes

PROCEDURE

1. Position players in the offensive third of the field.
2. Player A runs away from the ball, then checks back toward it and receives a pass from player B (see figure).
3. When player B touches the ball, player C runs to defend against player A.
4. Player A must create space to shoot using individual moves.
5. Player C is passive in playing defense.

KEY POINTS

Initially, space the server and the defender far enough apart so the offensive player has a distinct advantage. As players' skills improve, move the defender closer to reduce the time the attacker has to shoot.

RELATED DRILL

77

79   WALL PASS SHOOTING DRILL

PURPOSE

To develop abilities to create space for shooting with gamelike defensive pressure.

LEVEL

Intermediate, advanced

EQUIPMENT

One soccer ball and one goal for every four players

TIME

8 to 10 minutes

PROCEDURE

Level 1

1. Position players in the defensive third of the field (see figure).
2. Player A is the offensive player; player B is the defender.
3. Player A must pass to player C or player D as targets, then move to open space for a return pass and shot.
4. Player B should defend aggressively.

Level 2

1. The ball is served to player A.
2. Player A must collect the ball and take on the defender with individual moves to create space for a shot, or use players C and D for wall passes.

Level 3

1. Repeat level 2, procedures 1 and 2.
2. Add a goalkeeper to increase defensive pressure.

KEY POINTS

Encourage players to change speeds, using quick bursts to create spaces for shots.

RELATED DRILLS

None

80   1 V 1 FOR ALL DRILL

PURPOSE

To develop dribbling skills for creating space, with gamelike defensive pressure.

LEVEL

Advanced beginner, intermediate, advanced

EQUIPMENT

One soccer ball and two goals for every eight players

TIME

10 minutes

PROCEDURE

1. Arrange eight players as shown in the figure.
2. Player A dribbles toward goal 1 in an attempt to score.
3. Player B defends.
4. After player A shoots he becomes the defender, and player B moves approximately 10 yards to the outside of the goal he defended.
5. Player C, who is waiting on the side of the goal that player B defended, becomes the new offensive player.
6. She receives a pass from the goalie and dribbles toward goal 2, which is approximately 30 yards away, while player A defends.
7. After player C shoots, she becomes the defender, and so on.
8. If the defender steals the ball at any time, he becomes the offensive player.
9. The defending player always goes to the side of the goal he defended.
10. Players rotate from offensive player, to defensive player, to the side of goal.

KEY POINTS

This drill is very intensive. Limiting the number of players to eight will maximize the number of touches, yet allow for brief recovery periods. Present this drill initially with no goalkeepers, to make scoring easier. As players' skills improve, add a goalkeeper to increase the defensive pressure.

RELATED DRILLS

27, 29, 30

81 NEVER-ENDING 3 V 2 DRILL

PURPOSE

To develop decision-making abilities concerning passing choices, with gamelike defensive pressure.

LEVEL

Intermediate, advanced

EQUIPMENT

One soccer ball and two goals for every seven players

TIME

10 to 12 minutes

PROCEDURE

1. Place two goals approximately 30 yards apart.
2. Position players so that there are three offensive players in the middle of the field, ready to score against two defenders (see figure).
3. Position two defenders at each end of the field.
4. On the coach's signal, the three offensive players pass the ball until they get close enough to a goal to shoot.
5. The player who takes the shot then joins the two defenders from this goal to try to score against the two defenders at the opposite end of the field.
6. If a defender steals a pass, that defending pair goes on the attack with the person from whom they stole the pass.

KEY POINTS

The offensive players have a numbers advantage, so there should always be an open player. Encourage players to make switching and overlapping runs to create space. Challenge players by allowing them no more than two touches on the ball.

RELATED DRILLS

None

PURPOSE

To develop shooting techniques and tactics under various degrees of defensive pressure.

LEVEL

Advanced

EQUIPMENT

Four soccer balls, one goal, six game markers, twelve jerseys (six red, six blue)

TIME

20 minutes

PROCEDURE

1. Position four game markers in a straight line 10 yards apart and 30 yards from the goal. Place two additional markers to the side of each goal post (see figure).

2. Two players, one red and one blue, stand at each of the six markers. A goalkeeper is in the goal.

3. The drill begins with the red team on offense and the blue team on defense.

4. On the coach's whistle, the red player from marker 1 speed dribbles to the goal and shoots. The blue defender must start in a sitting position.

5. On the second whistle, the red player at marker 2 passes to the red player from marker 5, who has just made a diagonal run. The blue player at marker 2 does not defend against this pass. The red player from marker 2 then moves to support the red player from marker 5 in an attempt to have either player shoot. Blue players from markers 2 and 5 defend.

6. The same action is repeated at the third whistle by players at markers 3 and 6.

7. On the fourth whistle, the red player from marker 4 must take on the blue defender from marker 4 one on one. The red

player from marker 4 attempts to drive toward the goal and shoot.

8. Players return to their markers after they finish their tasks. When all players are finished, they rotate to the next marker (1 to 2, 2 to 3, and so forth; 6 rotates to 1).

9. When all players have completed the cycle, the teams switch offensive and defensive roles.

KEY POINTS

Players need to practice shooting from different angles under varying circumstances. Encourage players to use good visual skills to locate the position of the goalkeeper. Remind them that placement of the shot is more important than its power.

RELATED DRILLS

None

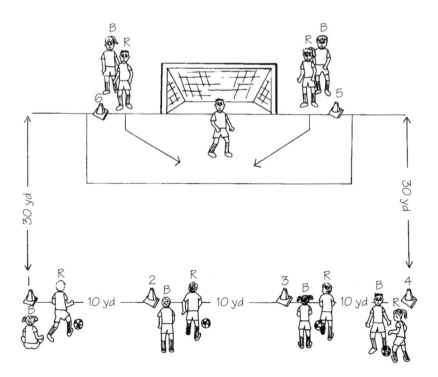

TARGET DRILL

PURPOSE

To develop combination play in the offensive third of the field.

LEVEL

Advanced

EQUIPMENT

One soccer ball, two game markers, one goal

TIME

20 minutes

PROCEDURE

1. Position two game markers 10 yards apart and 30 yards from the goal (see figure).
2. Players A and B take positions behind an imaginary line between the markers. Players C and D (target players) are stationed between the goal and the markers. A goalkeeper is positioned in the goal.
3. On the coach's signal, players A and B pass the ball back and forth as players C and D make various types of runs (lateral, switching, and diagonal) to open space.
4. Player A or B passes to player C or D.
5. Players C and D must execute a combination play (takeover, overlap, wall pass) before shooting.
6. Players repeat action several times and then change roles.

KEY POINTS

This drill is the first stage in developing combination play for use in the attacking third of the field. Encourage players to use vision, communication, and movement to develop creative play. Once players demonstrate an understanding of combination plays, make the drill more gamelike by adding one or two defenders. When using one defender, the first pass from player A or B must go to the target player being defended against. This drill can also be modified to develop the role of the third attacker by allowing either player A or player B to go forward, making a 3 v 2 situation. The player going forward should be the one who did not pass the ball forward (for example, player A passes and player B makes a run forward).

RELATED DRILLS

None

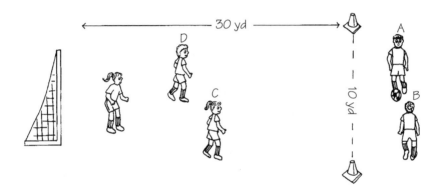

FRAMING DRILL

PURPOSE

To develop the ability to take shots from crossing balls

LEVEL

Advanced

EQUIPMENT

Four balls, two goals

TIME

20 minutes

PROCEDURE

1. Position players as shown in figure.
2. On the coach's signal player A passes to player B, who checks to the ball.
3. Player B passes back to player A, then pivots to the outside and runs down the sideline to receive a return pass (long ball) from player A. Player A then assumes the position at midfield that was just vacated by player B.
4. Player B dribbles the ball to the corner and crosses the ball.
5. Player 1, 2, or 3 attempts a shot off the crossing ball and then regroups for the next cross.
6. At the time player A starts the action on the right side of the field, player C starts the same action on the left side, passing to player D.
7. As soon as player A repositions herself at midfield, player E passes a ball to her.
8. After crossing the ball, player B runs to the corner where player C started, on the opposite side of the field, behind player F. Player C continues the action after player F has taken her turn. Player D, after crossing, runs to the corner where players A and E started the action.
9. After several crosses, players switch roles.

KEY POINTS

When positioning for crossing balls encourage player 1 to make a near post run, player 2 to position herself near the penalty kick line, and player 3 to make a far post run. Instruct players serving the crossing balls to serve flat passes for near post runs, waist-high balls for the penalty kick mark, and lofted balls for far post runs. Insist that players 1, 2, and 3 regroup quickly outside of the box as soon as one crossing ball is played, so they can time runs at proper angles for the next cross. Promote creativity by allowing players in the box to make switching runs. To create a more gamelike atmosphere, add one defender in the box at first, and then a second and third defender.

RELATED DRILLS

None

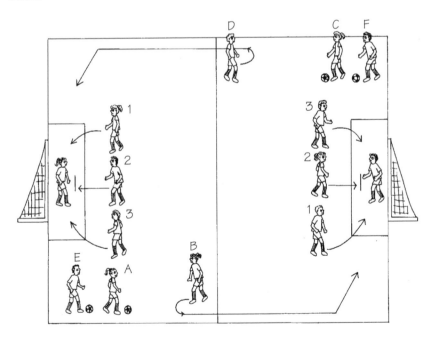

6

Game
Progressions

The progression of player development in games first focuses on skill acquisition and movement concepts. Limit the number of players in a game at first so that they have more time and space for making decisions. Such a limit ensures that each player gets more touches on the ball and helps make players more accountable for their choices, since there are fewer people to do the job. As players become more skilled and their knowledge base increases, the game progression adds more players, more rules, larger fields, and more team strategies. The process suffers when coaches emphasize competition too early, confuse players with soccer terminology prematurely, or implement burdensome rules and structure on beginners.

It would be impossible to discuss all of the changes in strategies, concepts, and so forth that occur at each level of learning. Instead, I will discuss some of the major concerns and recommend this series of game setups: 4 v 4, 5 v 5, 8 v 8, and 11 v 11. This sequence is not an original idea of mine. The Dutch developed this teaching model, which I have used as a guideline but have modified somewhat. The present progression varies somewhat from the one I used in my earlier coaching experience. I have adopted this model because it provides an easy transition from one level to the next for both players and coaches.

4 v 4

The 4 v 4, small-sided game works well for beginning players aged 5 and 6. Play this game on a field approximately 50 yards long by 30 yards wide. Goal size should be developmentally appropriate for the age and size of the players. I recommend a goal about 8 feet wide and 5 feet high. The rules of the modified 4 v 4 game are intentionally very simple. As a result, players can concentrate on the new skills and movement concepts they are learning without the burden of numerous rules.

Start the game with a kickoff, and use a kickoff after either team scores a goal. If a team kicks the ball out of bounds over the touchline, the opposite team receives a throw-in opportunity. If either team kicks the ball over the end line, the team whose goal is on that line gets a free kick. The nonkicking team must retreat to the half-field line, wait for the opposing team to take the kick, and then pursue the ball.

This 4 v 4 game changes the traditional rules for corner kicks and goal kicks. There are no goalkeepers. This adaptation is somewhat controversial among soccer coaches but allows teams to score many goals, reduces collisions, and diminishes injuries.

In front of the goal is a safety zone, similar to a goal box, which no one may enter unless the ball is there. If the ball is there, either team may enter. This rule allows the offense to finish a play and the defense to stop a scoring opportunity, but it prohibits the defense from camping in front of the goal. The game includes no offside rules or penalty kicks, and all penalties result in a free kick from the spot of the foul. To get the best results with this game, have eight players on the field and eight players on the sidelines. The eight on the field play for 5 to 7 minutes. Then the eight who were on the sidelines switch places with the field players. Children this age need a break after 5 to 7 minutes of continuous motion. The 4 v 4 model allows for continuous motion with hundreds of opportunities for collection and distribution. It also allows for numerous goal-scoring opportunities. The game should last approximately 30 minutes.

Collecting, Looking, and Decision-Making

The 4 v 4 game offers hundreds of opportunities to touch the ball. With only four players from each team on the field, players have the time and space to practice the process of distribution—collecting, looking, and decision-making. The coach should be on the field with the players, encouraging them to use this process. Initially, the players tend to engage in a kick-and-run style. With patient teaching of the distribution process, you will find that players demonstrate better use of space when in possession of the ball and that the game begins to have more structure. As players develop skills and the pace of the game quickens, the process changes to looking, collecting, and decision-making. Beginning players are not yet ready for this advanced progression. At the beginner level, coaches should allow some time in the game for the players to play without guidance.

Support and Balance

Players should be familiar with activities presented in this book that require them to move to support positions away from the person with the ball (open space) instead of moving to the space of the person who has the ball (closed space). The player who collects the ball must then look and make a decision about where to play the ball next. Coaches should emphasize proper spacing of supporting players to help eliminate a swarming effect around the ball. The four-player team model aids proper spacing. It aligns players in the shape of a diamond so that they may play the ball in any direction—forward, backward, or sideways (left or right).

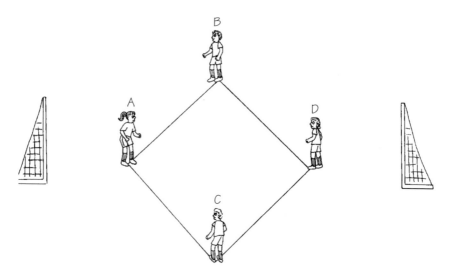

Figure 6.1   Single diamond shape.

As figure 6.1 shows, player A provides length, players B and C provide width, and player D provides depth. After the player passes the ball, he moves to a new support position. Continue to reinforce the concept of moving, both with and without the ball, while maintaining good team shape.

Maintaining the team shape (a diamond) helps ensure good field balance (spacing). I also recommend that coaches give players the opportunity to play each of the four positions in the diamond formation. Identify these positions and constantly refer to them by name during practice: forward, defender, right flank, left flank. Explain the roles of these positions simply. The forward stays near midfield when the other team has the ball (to provide length), and closer to her goal when her team has the ball. The flank players pinch toward the middle of the field and stay goal-side of their opponent when playing defense, but move outside toward the touchlines (to provide width) when on offense. The defender stays back near her goal when on defense (to provide depth) and moves forward when on offense (to provide support), but is cautioned to keep the team shape.

Remind beginners that defending is not the sole responsibility of the player in the back of the diamond, and that if everyone pushes forward on attack (swarming around the ball) the defense will lack depth. Using drills that require spacing of players (for example, the hello drill), teaching the roles of players in an uncomplicated fashion, and constantly referring to the names of these positions (forward, flank, defender) will hopefully reduce the swarming effect so prevalent within this age group. Be patient. It takes time for players to fully understand and demonstrate the notions of support and balance; however, they are critical building blocks for the next level.

5 v 5

The 5 v 5 game works well for players 7 and 8 years of age. It is the same game as 4 v 4—played on a 50-yard by 30-yard field, but with the addition of corner kicks and a goalkeeper. The goalkeeper may not come outside the safety zone, and no player is allowed inside the safety zone (even if the ball is inside the zone).

The goalkeeper adds new dimensions to the game. The attack must not only penetrate the defense but also beat the goalkeeper. The defense must reckon with the transition game after the goalkeeper collects the ball and initiates the attack. Give everyone who wants to experience the goalkeeper position a chance to do so. Not all children will want the opportunity because of the fear factor. Do not insist that these children play in the goal.

Teach only basic goalkeeping skills at this level. You should instruct goalkeepers to get their bodies behind their hands whenever possible and to position their hands correctly (thumbs in for balls above the waist, thumbs out for balls below the waist). They should catch and hold whenever possible, and position themselves at the proper angle to reduce the space from which an attacker can shoot. Continue to refer to the team shape (diamond) and positions of players (flank, forward, defender) during instruction.

8 v 8

Use the 8 v 8 game for players 9 and 10 years old. Play this game on a field approximately 70 yards long and 40 yards wide. Goals should be approximately 6 feet high and 12 feet wide. Each team has seven field players and one goalkeeper. Explain the role of each player during kickoffs, throw-ins, goal kicks, corner kicks, free kicks, and penalty kicks, since regulation rules apply at this level.

The addition of three more players than the previous level will challenge the players' ability, because they will have less time and space for technical execution and tactical decisions. The three players are added to the basic diamond shape—one as a forward, one as a defender, and one as a central midfielder—so that the team shape now has the appearance of two diamonds (see figure 6.2).

Players at this level should understand skill techniques and concepts of space and movement. Play is more structured, and you can

Figure 6.2 Double diamond shape.

expect more advanced results. Explain and discuss new concepts, such as the roles of various players:

- First attacker—the player with the ball, whose role is to penetrate the defense
- Second attacker—the teammate who is closest to the player with the ball and who provides support to him
- Third attacker—all other players who provide opportunities to gain space behind the defenders
- First defender—the player who pressures the opponent in possession of the ball
- Second defender—the player who defends against the opponent's second attacker and who is also responsible for supplying cover for the first defender
- Third defender—all other defenders who provide proper spacing and field balance
- Central midfielder—the player who provides a link for transition from defense to offense and who provides depth to relieve pressure on the forwards
- Goalkeeper—the player who defends against a variety of crossing balls and who helps relieve pressure on defenders during transition

Discuss how the role of the goalkeeper has expanded, since she is not confined to a safety zone (as in 5 v 5). Other topics to address include the relationship between the two forwards (combination play and spacing) and the relationship between the two defenders (spacing and support, in order to deny penetration and provide cover).

Team tactics are more complex at this level. Introduce more sophisticated attacking and defending tactics and set plays. Also, emphasize strongly the importance of using field width and diagonal movement in attacking tactics. Using the width of the field stretches the defense, which creates passing lanes. The defenders must choose between defending the width, which allows passing lanes on the inside, or compacting the defense, which allows passes to the outside. Diagonal movement, instead of only forward and backward movement, creates better visual space for players.

Creating better visual space opens up the field so that players may choose from several possibilities for penetrating the defense.

Introduce this age group to defensive team tactics. Tactical choices include which defensive scheme to utilize (zone, man to man, or a zone/man combination) and how to defend in different areas of the field (offensive third, middle third, and defensive third). As a rule, the closer the ball is to a team's goal, the more compact the defensive unit becomes.

Using Space Creatively

Players at this level are ready to explore the use of creative movements without the ball, including diagonal runs, lateral runs, overlaps, switches, and takeovers. Diagonal runs allow players to receive the ball with better vision (ability to see more of the field). They are effective at this level because players now have the ability to make longer passes. Such movements give the defense something different to look at and thus cause confusion. Players generally make vertical or diagonal runs to create space for themselves, and horizontal runs to create space for teammates.

You should incorporate into each practice session drills that emphasize using space creatively. These drills should include two-player combinations and plays involving more than two players.

A two-player combination can be simple, as when a player dribbles in one direction and a teammate comes from the opposite direction, takes the ball from him, and continues dribbling (a takeover). Another example of a two-player combination is a switch. Figure 6.3 shows a simple switch that you can use as a finishing drill. After player A collects the ball in the corner, he can cross the ball to player B, who is making a run to goal for a shot. There are also combinations of movement using more than two players. Figure 6.4 shows player B passing to player A, then player C running ahead and outside of player B to receive a pass from player A. This sequence is a three-player combination using an overlapping run by player C. Figure 6.5 shows a four-player combination. After player C collects the ball, she crosses to player D, who is making a diagonal run to the goal.

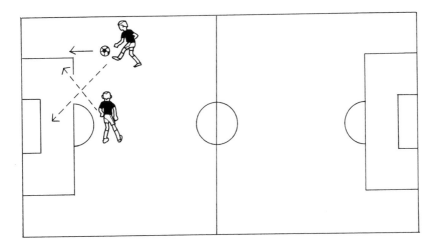

Figure 6.3 Simple switch.

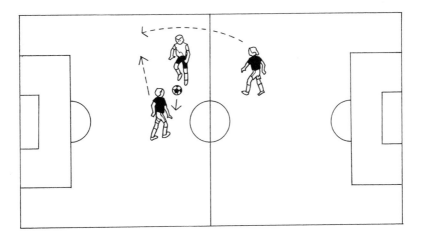

Figure 6.4 Three-player combination.

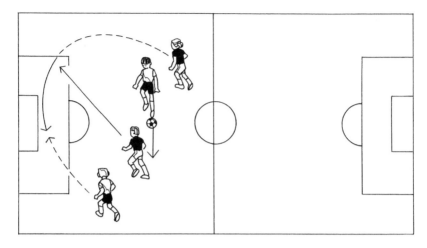

Figure 6.5   Four-player combination.

Set Plays

Coaches should introduce set plays at this level. Set plays contribute to greater structure in the game. When creating these plays, strive for simplicity. Complicated patterns of movement only frustrate players at this stage. Evaluate the players' abilities and design plays that they can execute successfully. Many game situations call for set plays, including kickoffs, corner kicks, goal kicks, direct free kicks, indirect free kicks, penalty kicks, and throw-ins.

11 v 11

By the time the players are 11 years old they should be ready to play on a larger field, approximately 100 yards long and 60 yards wide. The goals should be regulation size—8 feet high by 24 feet wide. The official rules of soccer apply at this level.

You should continue to review and refine skills and concepts taught at earlier levels. New skills and concepts presented at this level include more advanced individual skills, changes in roles and relationships when three players (forward, midfielder, and defender) are added to make a third diamond, the expanded role of the goalkeeper, the use of more players in set plays, and various systems of play.

Individual Skills

Emphasize technical skills such as long passing, heading, and individual moves with the ball. The players' size and strength will allow them to make long passes that were previously impossible. This ability adds a lot of diversity to their attacks. Always encourage them to make the longest passes possible without jeopardizing possession of the ball.

The players' ability to make longer passes also enables them to change fields quickly, which can devastate shifting defenders. Long passes allow them to cross the ball from the wing positions, thus developing the cross into a much more dangerous weapon.

Heading is another skill that should receive more emphasis at this level. By now players should have overcome most of their fear concerning heading. They should be aware that the ability to head the ball with precision allows them to maintain possession and increases scoring opportunities.

The repertoire of individual moves for creating space with the ball should expand at this level. Players need to continue to explore creative ways to change direction, speed, and level with the ball as well as to develop their own bag of tricks.

Support

Young players often practice offensive techniques and tactics only if they are designated as offensive players. The opposite is true if they are designated as defensive players. All players need to know, especially at this level, that they have both offensive and defensive responsibilities. Naming positions such as defender is only a way of identifying players for purposes of spacing and balance. There should be a team attitude that each player is a total player, capable of scoring when the opportunity presents itself or coming up with a big defensive play if that is what the situation demands.

Some coaches tell their defenders never to cross the midfield line for fear it will weaken the defense. Other coaches do not want their offensive players to recover to the defensive third of the field because it might affect a fast-break opportunity when they regain possession of the ball. And some coaches deny players the opportunity to make switching runs. In doing so they diminish or eliminate creativity and mobility in the attack. Instead, players should be given opportunities for more mobility. This does not suggest that teams should demonstrate reckless play, in an "anything goes" style. The key to having players become more mobile is maintaining field balance. For example, if a defender makes an overlapping run to a forward position to create a numbers advantage, teammates must provide depth on defense by shifting their positions accordingly. Coaches should teach players to play as a unit.

Retaining possession of the ball is still critical to the success of any team. The longer a team has the ball, the less chance the other team has of scoring. A factor that affects ball possession is the position of a player on the field and the risk factor associated with that position. Players who make lots of switching runs should be aware of the risk factors in each area of the field. Teach players in possession of the ball in the defensive third of the field to act swiftly to move the ball out of that area. Loss of possession in the defensive third is a critical situation. Warn players against excessive dribbling or dangerous passes, particularly in the middle of the defense third of the field. It is generally more acceptable to make longer forward passes in this area, even if they are not precise, rather than risk loss of possession and a scoring opportunity for the opponent.

Encourage players in the middle third of the field, however, to risk loss of possession by making penetrating runs or passes. Occasional loss of possession in this area is not as dangerous, because there is plenty of space in which to recover.

In the offensive third of the field, let players know that the more chances they take, the more they will score. Do not let your players develop mental blocks about shooting. Encourage them to take on defenders with their individual moves and to be aggressive in shooting. Loss of the ball in this area of the field will not be critical, as players have sufficient time to recover.

At this level, the addition of three players gives teams more flexibility in player movement. These three players (one forward, one central midfielder, and one defender) add a third diamond to the team formation (see figure 6.6).

Adding another forward player creates more opportunities to play the ball forward. It also increases the team's mobility, because

Figure 6.6 Triple diamond shape.

more creative movements are possible in the offensive third of the field. The extra central midfield player provides another target for teammates in the defensive third of the field, relieving pressure during transitions from defense to offense. The extra midfielder also provides support for the attacking players, creates scoring opportunities through combination play with the forwards, and provides defensive balance when the other central midfielder makes forward runs. The addition of the third defender provides more support for the goalkeeper and other defenders and helps the midfielder relieve pressure.

Goalkeepers must increase the level of their individual play at this level. Devote more practice time to goalkeeper preparation with drills that emphasize speed and reaction time. More specifically, these drills should involve variations on collecting, tipping, batting, diving, and clearing skills. The goalkeeper should also be involved in lots of small-sided game play during practices, in which players use communication, movement, collection, and distribution skills to relieve pressure from defenders.

Play Systems

To add more structure to the 11 v 11 game, coaches implement certain play systems or team formations. The system that a team uses reflects the philosophy of its coaching staff. The 3-4-3 system is one that players, using the progressions suggested earlier, learn easily. It provides opportunities for strong midfield and attacking play. However, coaches need to select a system flexible enough to accommodate the strengths of their players. Coaches should not make the mistake of using a system that does not suit their players.

For example, if a team has two very talented attacking players but is not as strong defensively, a coach may decide to use a 4-4-2 system. This system allows for an added defender, strong midfield players, and two attackers. The 4-4-2 system is a bit more defense oriented. Coaches using it should encourage players to interchange positions and to make supporting runs, thereby generating more offensive opportunities.

If a team has several strong midfielders, a 4-3-3 system may be appropriate. This system has four defenders, three midfielders, and three attackers, a pattern that makes it strong for defending and attacking but weaker in the midfield area. Strong play by the midfielders may compensate for this weakness.

Set Plays

The 11 v 11 game creates a situation in which there are 20 players, excluding goalkeepers, on the field. Therefore, when designing set plays to create scoring opportunities, spacing is a primary concern. All players should understand their responsibilities on each play, to help the team maintain proper spacing and not to become confused. The players at this level are bigger, stronger, and more highly skilled. Quick transition of the ball from one penalty area to the other is more likely. Coaches should not make the mistake of moving too many players forward in attacking positions during these free kicks. Such a maneuver makes the team vulnerable defensively, particularly if it occurs early in the game.

Remember that the progression from the beginning player, aged 5 or 6, to the player aged 11 or 12 is a long process. Always be fair to the players by giving them helpful information that is appropriate for their current level of ability. Above everything, be patient throughout this learning process.

7

Using Drills in Practice

Practices should include a variety of drills, activities, small-sided games, and full-field games. All of them promote the development of both individual and group skills and concepts, which in turn leads to improved strategies and games. Use drills as an integral part of practices to develop a small part of the big picture. Drills enable the players to focus on one aspect of the game without the distraction of other elements.

Careful planning will allow coaches to use drills that are appropriate for the players and offer many opportunities for both movement and ball touches. When planning, coaches should use drills to address specific areas of development. For example, if a team is having trouble scoring after moving the ball successfully to their offensive third of the field, then practices should include drills that emphasize finishing skills.

Making Practice Drills Successful

Several key factors make drills work successfully in practice. Plan to divide the group into smaller parts, change activities frequently, have sufficient equipment, vary formations, switch the order of activities, and make the drills gamelike.

Whenever possible, divide the players into small groups during drills. By using grids you can identify boundaries of general space for each group. In spacing grids, consider safety and your ability to observe adequately. Small groups of players within these grids will have opportunities for hundreds of touches on the ball during each practice. It is also a good idea to change combinations of players frequently so that everyone gets a chance to play with each other. Having small groups lets players accomplish more in shorter time periods, because there is less standing around. Coaches also have the opportunity to present more activities during each practice session.

In general, spend no more than 10 to 15 minutes on a particular drill during each session. Changing drills frequently helps players stay motivated, which increases their work rate. You must have sufficient equipment to implement lots of drills with smaller groups. Each team's equipment inventory should ideally include a couple dozen small-game markers of various colors, scrimmage vests, and a ball for each player. Small portable temporary goals are helpful for drills (in addition to regular goals).

Switching the order of activities occasionally helps drill work go more smoothly. For example, players can work on a drill involving individual moves the first part of the first three practice sessions. On the fourth practice session, you could start practice with a small-sided 4 v 4 game and follow with drills that help develop individual moves. Breaking practice routines keeps players motivated.

Changing formations regularly also gives a different look to drills. Alternately using triangles, squares, and circles for drill work adds variety. Varying the number of players, number of balls, and amount of space for drill work helps to promote a high work rate.

Probably the single most important factor in the success of a drill is whether or not the players are having fun. Drills will be fun for players if you present them in a gamelike fashion. Many of the drills in this book have these gamelike qualities. Using them in their proper progression not only helps players develop skills and concepts but also is enjoyable for them.

The practices designed on the following pages are broken down into age groups. The drills selected for each age group reflect the ability of the mythical "average" player of that age. You may feel, for example, that the drills designed for 7- to 8-year-olds are not appropriate for your particular team of 8-year-olds, because they are either too challenging or don't quite stretch your players' abilities. Modify them as necessary. Also keep in mind that the practices presented do not include designated times for water breaks and stretching. Schedule such times in your practice where appropriate.

Practices for 5- to 6-Year-Old Players

Practices for 5- to 6-year-old players should last approximately 60 minutes. Each practice should include a variety of drills, activities, and small-sided games that will promote the development of individual skills and concepts, group skills and concepts, strategies, and games. At this level, offensive skill and concept development is much more difficult than defensive development. Therefore, when organizing your practice plan, design drills that have no defensive pressure or passive defensive pressure. Always give the numbers advantage to the offense if there is a numbers differential, such as 3 v 1.

Develop a warm-up plan for your players. Follow this plan as players are arriving to practice. Include in the warm-up plan activities that involve various skills, including juggling, passing, dribbling, heading, and shooting. Players can do these activities without much coaching instruction. The players will tend to gravitate toward the shooting station. Encourage them to spend equal time at all the stations.

I recommend that at this level you use the 4 v 4 format for scrimmages. It is helpful to paint the goals different colors—for example, red and green. During the game, have one team wear green jerseys and the other team red ones. The painted goals give the players a visual cue for determining direction. If other groups use the goals and painting is not allowed, simply tie a couple of green shirts to the top of one goal and red shirts to the other. If the teams switch sides at a specified time, untie the shirts and place them on opposite goals. If a player or players on the team are color blind, use shirts with symbols.

You should not place players in this age group on regular teams. Regular teams mean competition. When competition is emphasized too early, the development of skills and concepts is minimized. Coaches should view competition for 5- to 6-year-old children like flu medication. If given in proper doses, it can be helpful. If given in too large a quantity, it can be harmful.

TABLE 7.1

5- to 6-Year-Old Practice

Type of Activity	Content	Time
Large-group skillwork	Monday morning traffic drill (#11)	5 minutes
Large-group skillwork	Fancy footwork drill (#17)	10 minutes
Small-group skillwork	Partner tag (#21)	10 minutes
Small-group skillwork	Thread-the-needle drill (#33)	5 minutes
Large-group instruction	Demonstrate diamond formation	10 minutes
Large-group game	4 v 4 scrimmage	20 minutes
Large-group instruction	Closure	5 minutes

Each week, when meeting with the players, divide the children differently so they experience playing with all the other children. Tables 7.1–7.3 show three examples of how you should organize a typical practice for 5- to 6-year-old children.

TABLE 7.2

5- to 6-Year-Old Practice

Type of activity	Content	Time
Large-group skillwork	Zigzag drill (#7)	5 minutes
Large-group skillwork	Fancy footwork drill (#17)	10 minutes
Large-group skillwork	Follow the leader drill (#18)	5 minutes
Large-group instruction	Review team shape (diamond)	10 minutes
Large-group instruction	Demonstrate diamond formation	10 minutes
Large-group game	4 v 4 scrimmage	20 minutes
Large-group instruction	Closure	5 minutes

TABLE 7.3

5- to 6-Year-Old Practice

Type of activity	Content	Time
Large-group skillwork	Volcano drill (#6)	5 minutes
Large-group skillwork	Fancy footwork drill (#17)	10 minutes
Small-group skillwork	Hello drill (#37)	10 minutes
Small-group skillwork	Partner stationary shooting drill (#68)	10 minutes
Large-group instruction	4 v 4 scrimmage	20 minutes
Large-group instruction	Closure	5 minutes

Practices for 7- to 8-Year-Old Players

Practices for 7- to 8-year-old players should last approximately 60 to 75 minutes. Continue to introduce them to skill techniques. Balance practices by including some drills that develop skill technique with no defensive pressure. Players within this age group are growing physically and mentally, so you can challenge them to incorporate more individualized team tactics into their play. The addition of a goalkeeper definitely changes both practice and game structure.

Scrimmages at this level should use the 5 v 5 format. This design uses four players in a diamond shape, plus a goalkeeper. Players at this level should be placed on regular teams. Encourage players to maintain the team shape during play. The emphasis during practice and game situations should be on long-term player development and not the short-term goal of winning. Tables 7.4–7.6 show three examples of practices for 7- to 8-year olds.

TABLE 7.4

7- to 8-Year-Old Practice

Type of activity	Content	Time
Large-group skillwork	Freeze drill (#20)	10 minutes
Small-group skillwork	Monkey-in-the-middle drill (#49)	10 minutes
Small-group skillwork	Run-and-shoot drill, level 1 (#71)	15 minutes
Large-group skillwork	Explain role of goalkeeper in 5 v 5 play	10 minutes
Large-group game	5 v 5 scrimmage	20 minutes
Large-group instruction	Closure	5 minutes

TABLE 7.5

7- to 8-Year-Old Practice

Type of activity	Content	Time
Large-group skillwork	Freedom drill (#19)	10 minutes
Large-group skillwork	Pendulum drill (#39)	10 minutes
Small-group skillwork	Open-corner drill (#70)	10 minutes
Large-group instruction	Explain role of flank players	10 minutes
Large-group instruction	5 v 5 scrimmage	20 minutes
Large-group instruction	Closure	5 minutes

TABLE 7.6

7- to 8-Year-Old Practice

Type of activity	Content	Time
Large-group activity	Circle collection drill (#36)	10 minutes
Small-group activity	Circle dribble tag, level 1 (#23)	10 minutes
Small-group activity	Pass-and-shoot drill (#73)	10 minutes
Large-group instruction	Explain role of forwards in diamond formation	10 minutes
Large-group game	5 v 5 scrimmage	20 minutes
Large-group instruction	Closure	5 minutes

Practices for 9- to 10-Year-Old Players

Practices for 9- to 10-year-old players last approximately 75 to 90 minutes. These players should have had previous experience playing 4 v 4 and 5 v 5.

Introduce the double-diamond 8 v 8 formation at this level. The game is more structured, and play should be intentional. Practice continues to emphasize the process of collecting, looking, and decision-making. Introduce and reinforce the defensive concepts of cover and compactness as they apply to both the individual and the team. Also, emphasize principles of offensive play such as supporting teammates and using field width, which will be integral in the development of more creative play at this level.

One of the most difficult concepts to teach this age group is how to deny space efficiently. Players at this level often feel that it is their responsibility to defend the entire field. They will follow any space the ball goes to. If there is an entire team of this type of player, there will likely be a swarming effect during play. To alleviate this situation, players must become aware of their particular field position and how it relates to other positions. At the same time, they must maintain the double-diamond team shape.

Continue to develop the skills and concepts that players ought to have learned at an earlier stage. If players do not possess these skills or understand the concepts, do not proceed until you establish a suitable foundation or offer an alternative for additional training.

Tables 7.7–7.9 show sample practice plans for 9- to 10-year-old players.

TABLE 7.7

9- to 10-Year-Old Practice

Type of activity	Content	Time
Large-group skillwork	Fancy footwork drill (#17)	10 minutes
Small-group skillwork	2 v 2 keepaway drill (#55)	10 minutes
Small-group skillwork	Wall pass shooting drill (#79)	10 minutes
Large-group skillwork	Explain double-diamond formation	15 minutes
Large-group game	8 v 8 scrimmage	20 minutes
Large-group instruction	Closure	5 minutes

TABLE 7.8

9- to 10-Year-Old Practice

Type of activity	Content	Time
Large-group skillwork	Four-grid scramble drill (#29)	10 minutes
Small-group skillwork	Partner dribble game (#27)	10 minutes
Large-group skillwork	1 v 1 for all drill (#80)	10 minutes
Large-group skillwork	Explain role of 2 forwards in double diamond formation	10 minutes
Large-group game	8 v 8 scrimmage	20 minutes
Large-group instruction	Closure	5 minutes

TABLE 7.9

9- to 10-Year-Old Practice

Type of activity	Content	Time
Small-group skillwork	Two-cone drill (#40)	10 minutes
Small-group skillwork	Check out–check in drill (#51)	10 minutes
Small-group skillwork	3 v 1 shooting drill (#76)	10 minutes
Large-group skillwork	Explain role of central midfielder in double diamond formation	15 minutes
Large-group instruction	8 v 8 scrimmage	20 minutes
Large-group instruction	Closure	5 minutes

Practices for 11- to 12-Year-Old Players

Practices for 11- to 12-year-old players should last approximately 90 minutes. Continue to develop and refine the players' individual skills and concepts. The physical changes in the players (size, speed, and strength) present new strategic opportunities. Practices include the exploration of creative solutions that adopt a more mobile approach to attacking the opponent's goal. This mobile approach calls for flexibility in the positioning of players, more complex concepts of width and support, and the introduction of new movement concepts.

Before you present these new opportunities, make certain that players have learned the skills and concepts at the 5- to 6-year-old, 7- to 8-year-old, and 9- to 10- year-old stages of development. If this progressive system has not been in place, go back as far as necessary in the development of skills and concepts to ensure that your players have a positive experience while learning. Tables 7.10 to 7.12 show some practice plans for 11- to 12-year-olds. Remember, these practice plans are just a sampling of the variety of experiences available for 11- to 12-year-old players.

The plans include time for an 11 v 11 scrimmage. Restricted team size often means that you will not have enough players for 11 v 11. If this is the case, employ the 8 v 8 format. Another possible solution to this problem is practicing with another team. You may even want to vary your schedule so you practice with several different teams.

Whichever age group you work with, try to remember that the players will spend considerably more time in practice situations than in games. Make the practices valuable and fun learning experiences that will keep kids coming back to enjoy another day of soccer with their friends.

TABLE 7.10

11- to 12-Year-Old Practice

Type of activity	Content	Time
Large-group skillwork	Three-team passing drill (#58)	10 minutes
Small-group skillwork	3 v 2 line game (#57)	10 minutes
Large-group skillwork	Never-ending 3 v 2 drill (#81)	10 minutes
Large-group skillwork	Explain the role of 3 forwards in the triple diamond formation	15 minutes
Large-group game	11 v 11 scrimmage	25 minutes
Large-group instruction	Closure	5 minutes

TABLE 7.11

11- to 12-Year-Old Practice

Type of activity	Content	Time
Large-group skillwork	Three-team keepaway drill (#60)	10 minutes
Small-group skillwork	Keepaway drill (#54)	10 minutes
Small-group skillwork	Two-teammate passing game (#56)	20 minutes
Large-group skillwork	Shooting combination drill (#82)	20 minutes
Large-group instruction	Explain the role of the 3 defenders in the triple-diamond formation	15 minutes
Large-group game	11 v 11 scrimmage	25 minutes
Large-group instruction	Closure	5 minutes

TABLE 7.12

11- to 12-Year-Old Practice

Type of activity	Content	Time
Large-group skillwork	Sprint challenge drill (#25)	10 minutes
Large-group skillwork	Six-goal game (#30)	10 minutes
Small-group skillwork	Shake-and-take drill, level 3 (#24)	10 minutes
Large-group skillwork	Explain role of 4 midfielders in triple-diamond formation	15 minutes
Large-group game	11 v 11 scrimmage	25 minutes
Large-group instruction	Closure	5 minutes

About the Author

Jim Garland has worked with children ages 5 to 11 as an elementary physical educator for 33 years. He also has over 15 years' experience coordinating summer soccer camps and clinics for Motion Concepts Summer Soccer Camps and has coached soccer teams from beginners to high school age.

As an undergraduate at Towson State University, Maryland, Garland earned Most Valuable Player awards for two consecutive years. In 1970, he was elected Senior Athlete of the Year. In 1985 he was inducted into the Towson State University Athletic Hall of Fame. Garland earned his masters from Morgan State University in Baltimore in 1978. He earned his doctorate from Nova Southeastern University in Fort Lauderdale, Florida, in 1999.

Garland is a member of the National Soccer Coaches Association of America and the American Alliance for Health, Physical Education, Recreation and Dance. In his spare time Garland enjoys fishing and playing golf. He and his wife Debra live in Street, Maryland.